New Voices in the Field

A joint publication of
The National Association of
Secondary Schools Principals
and
Corwin Press, Inc.

New
∧ Voices in the Field

The Work Lives of First-Year Assistant Principals

Gary N. Hartzell
Richard C. Williams
Kathleen T. Nelson

CORWIN PRESS, INC.
A Sage Publications Company
Thousand Oaks, California

For information address:

Corwin Press, Inc.
2455 Teller Road
Thousand Oaks, California 91320

SAGE Publications Ltd.
6 Bonhill Street
London EC2A 4PU
United Kingdom

SAGE Publications India Pvt. Ltd.
M-32 Market
Greater Kailash I
New Delhi 110 048 India

Printed in the United States of America

Library of Congress Cataloging-in-Publication Data

Hartzell, Gary N., 1943-
    New voices in the field: the work lives of first-year assistant
  principals / Gary N. Hartzell, Richard C. Williams, Kathleen T.
  Nelson.
      p. cm.
    Includes bibliographical references and index.
    ISBN 0-8039-6190-1 (alk. paper).—ISBN 0-8039-6191-X (pbk.: alk.
  paper)
      1. Assistant school principals—United States—Interviews.
  2. High schools—United States—Administration—Case studies.
  I. Williams, Richard C., 1933- . II. Nelson, Kathleen T.
  III. Title.
  LB2831.92.H38   1995
  371.2'012—dc20   95-792

This book is printed on acid-free paper.

95 96 97 98 99 10 9 8 7 6 5 4 3 2 1

Corwin Press Production Editor: Diana E. Axelsen

Contents

Preface

The purpose of this book is to give readers a sense of how it feels to become an assistant principal (AP) in today's secondary schools. It is built around stories new APs told us of what they experienced both personally and professionally during their first year. Their stories provide beginning administrators with an alternative and personal kind of understanding that makes this work different from other studies of the assistant principalship.

From 1989 to 1994, we engaged in formal and informal conversations in California, Washington, and Nebraska, with approximately 90 first-year secondary school APs. Our purpose in these discussions was to ask new assistants to share their perceptions of the events and emotions they experienced in the transition from teacher to administrator and the adjustments they had to make to this new, faster paced, and differently demanding professional world.

The stories we heard from new APs sort into varieties of experiences, and each of the book's chapters, except for the first two and the last, describes one of them. The first chapter sets the scene for the book by describing the experiences of one new assistant, whom we call "Maria Winston." The chapter is based on a diary kept by a beginning AP during her first year in a junior high school. Although the chapter does not describe every challenge Maria faced during her first year in office, every incident in the chapter was part of her individual experience. The second chapter puts Maria's story into context, describes the importance of the assistant principalship as the entry to administrative careers, discusses the invisibility of the assistant principalship in administrative literature, and more fully explains our purpose in writing the book.

Each of the succeeding six chapters traces a different theme in the new AP experience. Chapter 3 describes how measures of time and duty are different in the AP's office from what they were in the classroom. APs' duties include much more than appear in their job descriptions, and they find the pace of the assistantship faster, more unpredictable, and more relentless than in any other job they have ever had in education—more so, in fact, than most have ever had anywhere.

Chapter 4 describes adjustment to the most dominant feature of an AP's life: the administration of student discipline. Maria complained to her diary that discipline drained her time, energy, and emotional stamina far more than she ever expected it would, and every new AP we talked with who had any responsibility for building discipline confirmed her lament.

Chapter 5 describes the redefining of relationships with former colleagues. As much as they might like to retain the perception of teaching they had while in the classroom themselves, immediately on appointment new APs begin to see teachers differently and— equally important—are seen differently by teachers. The role of supervisor and evaluator causes significant and surprising changes in the personal relationships APs have with people they previously thought of as peers and colleagues.

Chapter 6 addresses a different relationship challenge. Instead of redefining an existing relationship, new APs are called on to create relationships with people they have never dealt with before at any significant level. For the first time, they work closely with a secretary and coordinate and supervise the work of other support staff. They begin to realize how clerks, custodians, and others contribute to the functioning of a school and how important it is to develop strong working relationships with them.

Chapter 7 shows that as beginning APs are initiated to their new peer group, they usually are made to feel welcome and wanted. But many beginning assistants are surprised to find that their principals and AP peers do not necessarily treat them the way they expected or fit the idealized models they were exposed to in their university training. Learning "the way we do things around here" through structured and incidental interactions with the principal and other assistants is an enlightening experience.

Chapter 8 umbrellas the chapters that come before it as new APs describe the emotional impact their experiences have on them.

Finally, Chapter 9 employs research on APs, organizations, and organizational sociology to explain four of the most common themes in the experiences of new APs as they were explained to us by those who lived them.

We use research results pulled from the literature of organizational socialization, communication, and interpersonal dynamics to support some of the speculations we make and the conclusions we draw. Although most of these studies were done in fields other than education, the diversity of occupations and settings in which they were conducted, many of which qualify as professional, is broad enough to support reasonable generalization. The processes of transition, uncertainty about new environments, and the nature of socialization are so much a continuing part of the human experience that the results of these studies are applicable to the experience of new APs.

Our approach in this book is reminiscent of the method Studs Terkel used so effectively in *Hard Times* (1970), *Working* (1974), and *The Good War* (1984). Drawing on the personal reflections of new APs, we hope to give a description of the experience in human terms. Terkel produced what he called books of memory, rather than books "of hard fact and precise statistic" (1970, p. 3). He talked with people about events that had defined their lives and asked them to share their experiences. The impressions he collected allowed readers to understand a little better the impact those events had on the people who lived through them. Reading cannot substitute for participation, but in retelling personal experiences, Terkel gave readers insights that could never be pulled from maps, figures, charts, or statistics. This book differs from Terkel's in many ways, but it shares the same basic intention.

Research across a wide variety of fields has shown that the shocks of a new job can be lessened and the chances of successful socialization increased by "realistic job previews" (Wanous, 1980). Our contention is that the most realistic job preview is a personalized picture of the job drawn in the words of those who have lived it. By sharing the impressions that APs have of the position and by reviewing research findings and theoretical concepts that place their experiences in a wider context, we seek to bring "to life" the complexities, ambiguities, sorrows, and joys experienced in the first-year assistantship.

About the Authors

Gary N. Hartzell is Associate Professor of Educational Administration at the University of Nebraska at Omaha. A former high school teacher, assistant principal, and principal in California, he received his doctoral degree from the University of California at Los Angeles and then joined the faculty of the University of Nebraska. His particular interest is in schools as workplaces for adults, and he is interested especially in the socialization of new administrators, particularly assistant principals. He is the author of *Building Influence for School Librarians* and a number of articles on administrator socialization and practice.

Kathleen T. Nelson is Assistant Principal at South Whidbey Island High School in Langley, Washinton. After completing a master's degree in English, she taught for 4 years before joining the faculty at Mira Costa High School in Manhattan Beach, California in 1972. She taught a variety of courses and then became Activities Director, a position she held for 3 years. In 1986, she became part of the guidance staff at the high school as an Educational Advisor, a restructured counseling position with extensive administrative duties. She began her career as an assistant principal at Mira Costa in the 1992-1993 school year.

Richard C. Williams is Professor of Education, Educational Leadership, and Policy Studies in the College of Education at the University of Washington in Seattle. He is also Director of the Danforth Educational Leadership Program, the administrator credential program at the College of Education. He received his doctoral degree from the University of Minnesota in 1966. From 1966 to 1990, he was Professor of Education in UCLA's Graduate School of Education, where he also served as a Director of the Seeds University Elementary School. From 1990 to 1994, he was the Executive Director of the Puget Sound Educational Consortium at the University of Washington. He also served one term on the school board in the Santa Monica-Malibu Unified School District in California and has consulted with several research organizations, universities and school districts. His publications have included books, monographs, chapters, articles, and papers on educational change, program evaluation, decision making, and educational leadership.

Maria's Story

*I could a tale unfold whose lightest word would harrow up thy soul, freeze
thy young blood . . .*

Shakespeare / Hamlet

Maria Winston parked her Honda in the green space marked
"Reserved for Visitors" outside the Education Building at the
university, twisted the rearview mirror toward her face, and assessed
the damage from the long Monday at her school. The day showed.
Ruefully, she remembered a time when it was important that her
lipstick was always fresh, her hair perfectly in place, her clothes
wrinkle-free. She sighed, ran her fingers through her short, permed
hair, pinched her cheeks for color, and straightened the bow on her
suit blouse.

When Professor Simpson had called, asking her to talk to his
summer secondary school administration class about her first year
as an assistant principal (AP), Maria had hesitated. Of course, she
was flattered, but it felt like a lifetime ago that she sat in one of these
modern brick and glass classrooms, eagerly offering her opinions on

educational reform, convinced that all she needed was a chance to take on the whole job herself. A year's experience had forced changes in some of her most passionately held beliefs about education and educators.

She remembered her first faculty meeting at Glenview Junior High, scarcely a week after her predecessor had accepted a principalship elsewhere and she had been selected to take the AP position. Maria had prepared an opening speech about curricular change, but most of the teachers were interested only in class size and textbook orders. It didn't take long for her to realize that putting administrative theory into practice wasn't going to be all that easy. Still, she recalled Simpson's class fondly. He had been the best of her professors; as a former school administrator, he brought a useful combination of professional experience and scholarship to his teaching.

She rounded the east side of the building and found him waiting for her. The year had not changed him: same pale face, broad smile, and gray hair. Maria thought she even recognized the suit.

"I'm so glad you could come," he said, grasping her hand with both of his. "There's nothing like on-the-job experience to help a group of aspiring administrators get a feel for what the job is really like."

"Do you really want me to tell them that? How detailed and graphic do you want me to be?" Maria laughed. "You do want some of them to go into administration, don't you? Or am I your secret screening device?"

"Just give them a reality check," Simpson said, leading her down a narrow corridor with classrooms opening on either side. The white linoleum and matching paint gleamed, and Maria flashed on the locker hallway back at school with its dingy cement floor. "It's a good group," Simpson was saying. "They're almost all teachers, though, and they need to know what it's really like in the AP's office. I can't find much research to give to them, so I've told them my war stories, but I've been away from it for long enough now that my credibility is starting to erode."

The room quieted as the two of them walked in. Thirty students, mostly women, mostly in their 30s, an ethnic salad of Whites, African Americans, Latinos, and Asians. Professor Simpson opened the class with a greeting, paused, looked at the students, and said, "Before we begin tonight, I'd like all of you to think about this basic question: Why do you want to be a school administrator?"

He had asked Maria's class the same question, and she remembered responding that she wanted to make a difference, break the old boy network, something like that. But one of the first things she had noticed in her new job was that the teachers, even close friends, treated her differently. They assumed she had become part of the network she'd really hoped to change.

Simpson's students were not sure how to react to his question. A few of them laughed, as if they hadn't really thought about an answer. Someone called out, "Money." Others shifted uneasily in their seats. Finally, one man spoke up.

"I want to have some influence over what happens at my school. I'm tired of some of the things that go on, and tired of complaining about administrators."

"You can do as well as the people you work for now? Is that what you're saying?" Simpson asked. The man nodded.

A woman in the back, dressed in green sweats, answered next. "You can't make any decisions at all unless you leave the classroom. I love teaching, but I can't stand how powerless I feel."

"Is it power you're after?" Simpson asked. "Power to do what?"

"Power to change things," she replied.

Another woman, middle-aged, nodded agreement. "I love teaching, too, but I want to do more. People seem so narrow-minded. I want to be an administrator who supports teachers, who places more of a value on instruction than on athletics."

Murmurs of approval greeted this comment, and Maria felt the push-pull of their eagerness and her year of experience that had tempered her own naïveté and blind optimism. She, too, had wanted power, and she had seen herself in the principal's office wielding it.

Simpson smiled at the class as if he couldn't hope for a better warm-up audience. Then he introduced Maria. As he described her background—10 years as a classroom teacher, then several years as an in-service specialist who trained teachers in cooperative learning techniques and the writing process—Maria looked out over the faces in the audience. Because she had been one of them not too long ago, she understood what they needed, but she wasn't too sure she could give it to them. And she wasn't too sure they would want to hear, let alone believe, some of the things she was going to tell them.

Professor Simpson finished, and the class turned to Maria expectantly. "A year ago, I sat where you're sitting, and if someone had told me what I'm going to tell you this afternoon, I'm not sure I would have believed them. If I had, though, my rookie year might have been a lot easier. I thought I knew what went on in the office all day, but to tell you the truth, I didn't. My first year was filled with surprises. It was challenging and frustrating and crazy and exciting all at the same time. Some of what happened will sound really negative and discouraging, and it was, but I don't want you to think that I'm sorry about becoming a school administrator or that I'd think about leaving it. This last year was the most exhilarating year of my professional life so far. Being an assistant principal is fascinating— once you make sense of it."

Maria gave a brief overview of Glenview Junior High, a year-round school of 1,600 representing various ethnic groups crowded together on a campus designed for 1,000. "But," she said, "the school's not really the important thing. In one way, there isn't any such thing as a 'typical' school, and in another, they all have a whole lot of things in common. And I found out it's the same with assistant principals. There just isn't any such thing as a typical AP. I talk with other APs in our district, and they're not doing the same things I'm doing; the woman I replaced didn't even do the same things I'm doing—except for discipline. We all have discipline. And we all do a wide variety of other things; all of our job descriptions are long. The kicker, of course, is that line at the bottom that says 'and other duties as assigned.' That's really what an assistant principalship is all about.

"I know the books you're reading don't say much about the assistant principalship, if anything at all, and what they do say makes it sound like a mini-principalship: curriculum and instructional leadership, planning, that sort of thing. Well, it isn't. I don't do what the principal does. I'm supposed to have set duties, but the truth is that I spend my time handling whatever comes through the door—then I do my official duties when I can.

"Today, I want to try to help you understand what your first year is going to be like, what you're going to face when you go into the office. It's so different from teaching. I learned more last year than I learned in any other year of my life so far—with the possible exception of when I got married."

The class laughed, and Maria went on. "I kept a diary last year." She held up a thick three-ring binder with yellow Post-it notes marking certain pages. "I thought I'd share some of it with you. Dr. Simpson was always after us to document things. So, I started sorting through it after he called, and I've picked out some of the most memorable experiences from last year.

"As I reread my entries, several things occurred to me, and I want to organize my thoughts around those." Maria paused, looked down at her notes, and then said, "The first discovery I made was that I never knew so much was going on in the school while I was teaching. The safe, controlled environment in my classroom was deceptive, in a way. In the office, I saw things I was never aware of when I taught.

"They ranged from all kinds of little things to big ones. The opening of school, for example. I didn't realize how much work there was to opening school. I mean, when I was teaching, I came in a week or so early and got my room set up and got my books ready and everything, so I was ready to go when the students got there.

"Have you ever watched registration at your school? Worked at it? It's a big job! I didn't realize how much paperwork there is and the number of problems that have to be solved on the spot. Or how hard the secretaries work. You can't believe the activity level. I was really impressed."

Maria looked at the class. It was hard to read what they were thinking, but she could see they were listening.

"The office is a busy place. That may sound obvious, but I didn't have any idea how busy. The phones ring all the time. Students are always in the office. Some of them are sent by their teachers; some come on their own; some are brought in by the monitors. In a school Glenview's size, there's always something going on and somebody always has a problem. Lots of times, the problems are nickel-and-dime things, but sometimes they're not—and they're different problems than you see in the classroom.

"Assistant principals do as much counseling as anybody in the school, I found out—and I'm not a counselor. I never have been, never had any formal training, but some of these kids need help, and you can't just enforce the rules and walk away."

She told them about Sarah. Maria recalled the October day vividly. She'd been trying to finish up an observation report on a particularly interesting math class she had visited the day before. Her secretary told her that the PE teacher needed her in the gym to help a hysterical eighth-grade girl. The teacher had confronted the girl about her terrible attendance record, and the girl had started sobbing uncontrollably. Maria hurried down and found Sarah sitting, sniffling, in the PE office. In her gym shorts and T-shirt, she didn't look older than 10 or 11. Her round, pudgy face, sprinkled with pale freckles, was reddened from crying.

Maria was annoyed to be pulled away from working on a report that she had to get done by sixth period. It was always that way. She would just get into a project when something would interrupt her. Most of the time, it was discipline; sometimes it was a parent; frequently it was a teacher. This time, she expected the typical story of a boyfriend who didn't like her or a girlfriend who was gossiping about her. She didn't expect what Sarah finally blurted out.

"I know I've missed a lot of school. I told my mom that I was having bad cramps, but I really had another miscarriage, and this one was worse than the last one."

"The last one?" Maria stared at this little girl who looked as if she still played with dolls.

"I had one last summer, so I knew what it was this time. I couldn't come to school. It hurt too much. Anyway, my parents are gone all day anyway, so they don't care."

Maria was stunned, but in a moment her heart went out to Sarah. What do you say to a child like this? How could this be happening? What would she say to the teacher who would want to know what Maria was going to do to get this youngster to school more regularly? Maria felt both compassionate and helpless.

After Sarah calmed down, Maria returned to her office, trying to think of where she could get professional counseling help for the girl. She walked in and found that two teachers had sent students to see her. "Oh, Jason, not you again," she sighed as she recognized the first one. Jason had become disrespectful when Mrs. Klein insisted he stop talking to the girl next to him and pay attention. The second was also a boy. Andy hadn't brought his textbook to class for the second day, and Mr. Murphy had ordered him out of the class until he had it.

Jason was going to get to her, she decided. He picked his targets. He would be rude and unruly with one or two of his teachers and never a problem with the rest. On some days, Maria suspected that the classroom management styles and classroom demeanors of his teachers were more at the root of his pattern than his personality. On other days, she decided that he was just a shark who pressed an advantage whenever he sensed weakness. Jason got a quick lesson in manners, an hour of detention, and a chance to listen to the phone call to his mother, warning of more serious consequences if it happened again.

While Maria was talking with Andy and wondering whether some pathology lay behind adolescents forgetting textbooks, the telephone rang. The accounts clerk in the district office wondered whether she could straighten out a purchase order that didn't seem right.

Maria called her secretary, Gloria, and asked her to see what she could find out about the purchase order. Gloria came in a minute later with a file and said the problem was nothing and that she would take care of it. Maria said, "Thank you," but was thinking, "What a godsend you are." In a very short time, Maria had learned how valuable people like Gloria were. Gloria had taught her the range of duties her office covered and the ways to shortcut the system. She also buffered her boss from all sorts of problems, calmed down irate parents and teachers, and saw that the correspondence going out of the office was flawless. Maria recognized how much Gloria and others of the classified staff, like Tom the custodian, made her look good.

As Andy, the bookless boy, left for the textbook room, the hall monitor brought in a girl who had been discovered smoking in the west hallway rest room. Maria realized that the teacher observation report wasn't going to be done by sixth period. By the time she could deal with this student, the bell would ring for lunch, and she would be off to supervise the cafeteria. She would decide then whether to cancel the appointment with the teacher or just to speak from her notes.

As Maria oversaw the lunchroom, she looked calm enough, but her mind was racing. She wondered why the teacher couldn't have handled Andy's textbook problem himself. Jason merited attention, and the smoking girl she knew she had to deal with, but she wondered whether there were stories behind the behavior problems of these two, as there had been behind Sarah's.

Mostly, she thought about Sarah. Sarah's case showed Maria how complicated absenteeism could be. Sometimes it was just irresponsibility on the part of students or parents; some kids really were chronically ill; others just couldn't resist the lure of the streets and gangs. But sometimes absenteeism was only a small symptom of a much bigger problem—a problem like Sarah's, about which the school could do very little as an institution and about which Maria could do almost nothing as a person. She didn't tell Simpson's class, but she made Sarah one of her "projects," checking on her periodically, very quietly making sure she got certain teachers the next semester. Sarah's plight weighed on Maria's mind, but she saw so many seemingly squared-away youngsters every day that she thought of Sarah as the great exception.

By November, she knew that Sarah was not. Julie was an even sadder case. Maria had called her in to discuss frequent absences and failing grades. She had been a good student in the seventh grade but was now barely passing her academic classes. She had just returned from a 5-day absence. She walked into the office, nervously clutching her books to her chest as if they provided some kind of shield. With a little prodding from Maria, who wouldn't buy stories of broken-down cars and ill health, she poured out a chilling story.

Julie's boyfriend, Wayne, a high school sophomore, had thrown a bottle at a party, hitting a girl who lost her eye as a result of the injury. The girl's brother came after Wayne, shot him through the eye, killing him, and then cut off his fingers. Julie was terrified that the brother might come after her next. Maria tried to absorb the horror of this event and thought it was a wonder that Julie made it to school at all.

Maria looked out over Simpson's class, letting Julie's story sink in. "I found out quickly that the school is so much more than an instructional program. Students are involved in this complex web of relationships." She ticked them off on her fingers: "Schools, families, friends, neighborhoods. Sometimes they are supportive, but more often than you can imagine, they are dysfunctional and work against what you're trying to accomplish as an assistant principal."

A woman in the back raised her hand. She wore half-glasses attached to a bright red cord, and she peered at Maria over the top of the black frame. "But the schools can't do everything, solve every social problem. We're trained as educators, not cops or social workers."

Maria smiled, sympathizing with the woman and thinking of her own frustration. "That's true. I didn't want to do this either. I thought I was going to work on improving instruction. That's what they said when I got the job. They said they'd really chosen me because of my background. But I can't get to instruction the way I want to. The best teacher in the world can't get to Julie if she's got things like that on her mind. But you have to deal with the kids as they are, not as we'd like them to be. What are you going to do if you have a student tell you something like that?

"And they're going to tell you things like that. And other people are going to tell you things about students that you don't have any idea about. You'll find out who is seeing a psychologist or has a drinking problem, who has a parole officer, or who is gay, who has abusive parents. You start dealing with the parents, and you can learn a lot about the child. And I'm not talking about academics. I'm talking about their behavior and their attitude, the things that affect their academics. And I haven't even mentioned staff members yet. You're going to have some heavy things to deal with there too."

Maria looked at the woman and, as gently as she could, said, "You're going to be a counselor whether you want to be or not. And you're going to be a cop. The teachers expect it of you. The parents expect it of you. Even the kids expect it of you. You're going to be. And you're going to be dealing with real cops. And glad to do it.

"One thing I've learned is how to work with other agencies like the police. You'll find they can be your most valuable allies. Sometimes you have to call them to respond to a crime, like rape or drugs or weapons on the campus. Sometimes you just want advice, like how to collect evidence or when to press charges. The officers I've dealt with, especially the juvenile officers, have been competent and helpful. The fact is, we're all in this together, and we have to learn to share resources and work together. I never realized how much law there is in schooling. It's pervasive.

"And it isn't just the police. You will be working with Social Services and with parole officers and child abuse programs and welfare.

"You'll get frustrated because their clock doesn't tick the same as yours. You'll have a student in front of you who needs something right now, and they can't get it for you right now. It's hard. But you'll think of something."

A middle-aged woman in the front cleared her throat and twisted around in her desk to face the class. "I used to be a case worker for the Department of Children's Services. I sometimes would get calls from schools, but I had a caseload that wouldn't quit, and school problems weren't exactly a priority. It's not that you don't want to do some good—you're just overwhelmed by the system. What do you think I'm doing here?"

A flutter of laughter ran through the class. Maria smiled and nodded. "There is help out there. It's just sometimes hard to find."

Maria looked at her notes and then up at the class. "Sometimes it's not the outside agencies that are the problem—it's your own staff. And people you wouldn't expect it from. Everybody knows that good teachers are overworked and underpaid, and most teachers are dedicated to the point of self-sacrifice. When I was a teacher, I guess I assumed that all teachers were like that. I don't think that anymore.

"You are all here because you're self-selected. You're probably really good teachers. But not everybody's like you. And it's an eye-opener to discover that. How many of you have spent any time in another teacher's class recently? How many teachers in your school have you seen teach? Just a few, if any. Right?"

Nods of agreement.

"As an AP, you're going to go into teachers' rooms and see them teach, and you're going to have students tell you what they're like, and you're going to have parents complain to you about them. You're going to have to deal with them when they send you a student for discipline, or you'll be involved in a conference with them and the parent when the kid gets in trouble. You're going to see people in a very different light than you do when you're in the classroom. Sometimes they're better than you ever imagined, and sometimes they're just terrible.

"In the last year, I've witnessed some teachers' actions that have been way out of line—simply indefensible." As soon as the words were out, Jack Castle's face popped into Maria's mind. No one could remember exactly how long he'd been at Glenview. Maybe that was because he looked as if he had been built along with the school, sharing the same anonymous, early fifties style with his square, pragmatic body, Ozzie Nelson clothes, and bland features. But that face hid a surprising meanness. Every year, he picked out a few kids to exercise it on until, finally, one of the students would try to lash back. That's when Jack would send the offender to the office and demand that the student be removed from his class. If the counselor or AP did not respond fast enough to suit him, Jack let the whole staff know about it in the faculty cafeteria. "They're all soft," he'd say. "If we're not careful, they're going to let the inmates run the asylum."

Maria had learned from Jack and others like him that the rule "Always support teachers" had about the same validity as the maxim "The customer is always right." Her philosophy had evolved to a commitment to listen to both sides and then to make the best decision based on the information available. Unfortunately, that sometimes raised more questions than it answered. Just who are the AP's clients? Do some, such as teachers, deserve more support than others? Who gets the benefit of the doubt in a conflict? She still did not know the answers. She felt trapped. She was a fair person, but she also knew she needed continuing teacher support to accomplish myriad other goals. The contract could not force teachers to give the time for the extra activity and committee duty that kept important programs going and growing; alienating them was costly to the students and to the school. Issues did not seem as clear, she decided, as they had when she was in the classroom.

"Another way my perspective shifted when I left the classroom has to do with testing. Of course, I support the idea of student accountability. When I taught, I prepared my kids for the district standardized tests, and I thought I knew how political those results can be." Maria glanced in Professor Simpson's direction. She knew he shared her feelings on this topic. "But I didn't really know. The test scores show up in the newspaper, and people make judgments about your whole system on the basis of the numbers they see in the paper.

"Of course, it's more complicated than that. When I was teaching, I just gave the tests. It was an inconvenience and took time away from what I was supposed to be teaching, but I didn't have to do much. You know, I just stood there: 'Now, you read the directions silently while I read them aloud.' . . . But, did you ever really look at those tests and then look at your kids? I had to do that in preparation for a report to the board on our results. I spent an entire Sunday afternoon looking at question and answer patterns. More and more, I've developed serious reservations about whether our current tests reflect student learning."

She recalled reading through the district's competency test last year and coming across a reading selection about Egyptian obelisks. Students were supposed to read it and then write a composition about the importance of obelisks. Nowhere in the school's curriculum were obelisks mentioned, much less studied. Many of the students at Glenview were children of migrant workers, and it was unlikely that they would have picked up this information casually, yet their "competency" depended on it. Maria knew students who saw the word *obelisk* and put their pencils down because they had no idea what the word referred to. How could these students be held accountable for information that they could not access? It made Maria furious.

One particular incident showed how devastating this kind of system could be. Glenview had triplet girls in the eighth grade—Abby, Beth, and Catherine. Their parents had named them alphabetically in their birth order. At the June graduation ceremony, they were dressed alike, as usual, this time in white dresses and silver necklaces, their long, dark hair falling loosely around their shoulders. They came into the auditorium together. Catherine and Beth hurried to their places on the stage with the other graduates, but Abby walked to a seat in the audience with her parents.

Maria knew without looking at the program that only two of the girls were graduating. Abby had failed the competency test. On her second try, she had missed passing by three points, and district policy dictated that all students must pass the competency test in order to graduate. There is something wrong with a system that does that, she thought.

It was another issue of competing values for Maria. Achievement had to be demonstrated, but how could the demonstrations simultaneously be made valid and fair and efficient? She thought the whole movement toward authentic assessment was a giant step in the right direction, but her district administrators argued that they did not have the time or the resources to revamp the testing program. Meanwhile, children like Abby were labeled "incompetent." Maybe she was, or maybe she just did not know about obelisks.

The class was silent after Maria finished telling them about the triplets. She glanced at her notes and saw the word *TIME* written in capitals. "I'd like to think that the best minds in our district could design a better assessment system. Unfortunately, change is slow, and the other demands can be overwhelming. More than anything else my first year, I was surprised by the number of things that needed my attention. I was told when I took the job that principals were tyrants, but when it comes to tyranny, principals can't hold a candle to the clock."

At first, Maria thought that by applying all the principles of good time management to her new position—setting priorities, devoting chunks of time to different tasks, focusing on the task at hand—she could get a handle on the job. But more than any other position in the school, the AP has to be ready to respond to any problem that comes up.

"That's one of the things about this job that will really surprise you. I don't know how you feel about your teaching day, but my day just flies. I mean, I look at the clock and it's 7:30. The next time I look up, it's noon. When I look up again, it's 4:00. You won't believe it until it happens to you, but it's wildly different from the classroom. The priorities always seem to be set by others. I can't control my day. The truth is I can't control an hour. And discipline is just a black hole when it comes to time."

She told the class about one particular incident last winter. The school buses had picked up the students as usual at 3:00, but about 10 minutes later, one of the buses rolled back into the school parking lot. The driver refused to move unless the AP was called in. Maria was summoned, and she climbed onto the bus to find a furious driver, a young woman new to the district, and 30 watchful seventh and eighth graders. The bus stank, and rancid wisps of green smoke drifted around the seats like a special effect in a low-budget horror movie.

"One of these guys set off a smoke bomb on my bus, and I'm not leaving here until something is done about it." She pointed one long red nail accusatively toward the rows of seats behind her.

Maria turned toward the passengers and recognized the familiar signs of a conspiracy of silence. Heads down, eyes glued to the floor. Sure enough, as she started down the aisle, questioning students, no one had seen or heard anything.

Sighing, she turned back to the driver. "Look, it's 3:30. These kids have to get home, and you have another run to make. I'll take the names of all the kids and deal with this tomorrow."

Then she faced the students. "You're going to go home now, but I don't want you to think this is over. I know no one wants to tell on anyone else, but someone did a dangerous and destructive thing here, and I'm going to find out who it was. Think about that tonight, because I'm going to talk to all of you tomorrow." Heads and eyes were still averted, but they were listening.

The driver seemed mollified, and after Maria had gathered the list of names, the bus headed out of the lot.

The next morning, 5 minutes into first period, Maria started questioning students singly and in small groups: Where were you sitting? Who was sitting near you? What were you doing when this happened? Who is responsible? These were not the smooth maneuverings of Perry Mason interrogations. The students were nervous but reluctant to talk. It took a lot of time to chip away at their natural tendency to close ranks, but by 3 o'clock, she had a name.

During the next 2 days, Maria reconstructed exactly what had happened and suspended two culprits. After numerous calls, she finally had been able to contact their parents and arrange for follow-up conferences. Then she had filled out all of the necessary reports. Meanwhile, school life went on. Four students were sent up by teachers and had to sit outside her office, waiting for attention; pink While-You-Were-Out phone call slips piled up on her desk; she visited with a recently divorced parent new to the area who had come to school to enroll her daughter; attended a district attendance policy revision committee meeting; and rescheduled a teacher observation. But she knew she had to deal with the bus incident promptly. The bus driver, like many of the classified employees, viewed the AP as the "thin blue line" between the rights and dignity of the classified employees and the students they served.

Some problems, such as stink bombs, fights, injuries, thefts, food fights, maintenance breakdowns, emotionally distraught people, drugs, and weapons, require immediate attention. Others can wait. Like a triage physician, an AP learns to distinguish between emergencies and lesser ailments.

At least once, Maria had made the wrong diagnosis. She had been in her office, working on a report on test scores for an upcoming board meeting and trying to couch the bad news in the most diplomatic way possible. Suddenly, a girl appeared at her door to say that she was "needed" in the girls' bathroom. Maria decided to finish the thought she had started and then give some directions to Gloria before heading down the hall.

When she got to the bathroom, she found a frail eighth-grade girl curled up on the floor, hyperventilating. Maria dispatched another student to the office, with instructions to tell the secretary to call 911, and then attended to the girl. The student pulled through, but a delay of another few minutes might have been serious, even fatal.

Maria shuddered at the memory and then turned her attention back to Dr. Simpson's class and downshifted to more mundane concerns. "I can't even begin to tell you about the million little things that take up your time. There are discipline referrals for everything from not doing your homework to making rude noises in class to being under the influence. There's the endless paperwork. With everything else going on, the paperwork, of course, waits for the weekend.

"We're running out of time," Maria said, "but there are a couple of other things I want to tell you about." She paused, thinking about how best to use her remaining minutes. "I told you that when I was in the classroom, I never really knew what went on in the office. I realize now that that's exactly the point in a well-run school. Good administrators make sure that teachers can do their jobs, and most of the time, teachers aren't aware of even the serious problems occurring right under their noses."

One of those incidents happened on Maria's very first day as an AP. She was walking back to her office after bolting a lunch of food left over from the regular lunch period. George Palmer, another AP who was a veteran of 30 years in the district, called to her solemnly from across the quad. He had cultivated the authoritative voice of a television news anchor—it rumbled from down deep in his chest and struck fear into students. Sometimes he had the same effect on Maria. "Please come with me to witness something," he intoned.

He led Maria to the doorway of Room 23, where he called a student named Eric outside. Eric was a meek-looking eighth grader, not an inch over 5 feet, skinny, with closely cropped brown hair and sporadic acne.

"Do you have something in that backpack that I would be interested in seeing?" Palmer thundered.

Eric started to shake his head, looked at Mr. Palmer, thought better of it, and unzipped his backpack. Inside was a black and silver handgun. Loaded. Maria went weak-kneed looking at it.

The boy went quietly with them back to the office, almost as if he were relieved at being caught. When they got inside, he broke down.

"These high school guys said they were going to get me. They were going to wait for me after school. I took my dad's gun to scare them. That's all I wanted to do. I've never even shot it." He looked at the gun as if it were some alien being that had crept into his backpack.

Maria could not help but feel sorry for him. He had no discipline record but had managed to antagonize an older group of students whose names he didn't even know. Many students seemed to be imitating patterns of violence they saw on television and in movies. Maria knew that Eric would be arrested and then expelled, and he should be. Nonetheless, the incident alerted her to the ambiguities and conflicts inherent in many discipline cases. This was not a hardened gang member, but a scared child who did not think about other options and who had easy access to a weapon.

Throughout the year, Maria had stumbled on to a number of youngsters who were trying to make their way in an increasingly violent and disturbing world. She remembered Tony, a shy young Mexican American who was into heavy metal. He liked to wear shirts depicting graphic violence, like screaming human skulls dripping blood. His English teacher had been concerned about the pictures he drew in his journal—brutalized bodies: beaten, shot, mutilated. He was sent up to see Maria, journal in hand.

She looked through the drawings, page after page of them, many of them colored red and green, all of them drawn with meticulous detail. Then she looked at Tony, who shrank away from her in the gray tubular chair across from her desk. "Why do you draw these pictures, Tony? Is that really how you feel?" she asked.

"I don't know," he mumbled.

"What about this one?" Maria turned the notebook toward him. The page featured a particularly disturbing drawing of a man lying down, his legs and arms apparently burnt off—smoke still rising from the stubs. There was a metal pipe pushed all the way through the man's head. The caption read: "Death by Pipes."

"Tony, have you ever seen anything like this picture?"

Tony said nothing at first but gave Maria a look of infinite sadness, much too old for a 13-year-old boy. Tears slid down his cheeks.

Finally, he started to talk. "My dad picked me up at my friend's house, and he was stopped by the cops. This was last year. They thought he was drunk. They asked him for an ID, but he didn't have one, so they beat him up. My uncle lived near there, and he tried to help my dad, but they beat him up too. They hit his head on the cement. He was just lying there bleeding, and I thought he was dead. I saw this pipe on the ground, and I picked it up. I hated them, all those cops, so I threw the pipe at 'em as hard as I could." Tony stopped, tried not to cry, but couldn't help himself. He rubbed angrily at his eyes.

"It's okay," Maria said. "What happened then?"

"I don't know. I ran away."

All of the fear and anger and hatred of the past year poured out of him as he gave in to sobbing. He was afraid the police were looking for him. He couldn't tell anyone about this. For months, his only outlet had been the drawings in which he re-created that grisly scene over and over.

Maria tried to comfort Tony as she thought of her own middle-class upbringing and sheltered childhood. Nothing in her past or in her education had prepared her for Tony. She was finding a lot of things for which her experience and her education had not prepared her.

Students were not the only ones who did not always behave according to the rules. Maria related the story of the teacher who had been complaining about break-ins and a horrible smell in her classroom. At first, the administration and the custodial staff took her seriously. Then she started locking her classroom door during the day and pulling down the shades to protect her students from the "evil" people trying to get in. Before long, it was clear that the problems were not outside, but inside the teacher's head. The most disturbing part of the story was the fact that a number of faculty members knew about her bizarre behavior but did not think it was their responsibility to report it.

"I like to think that the adults are the people in charge and that if we all get together, we can help students solve their problems." Maria paused, "But sometimes, the adults *are* the problem."

She told the class about the two mothers she had invited into her office to discuss a dispute between their daughters. The two women started off amicably enough, but within 5 minutes they were at each other's throats and Maria had to call in another administrator to get them out of her office. The class laughed, and then Dr. Simpson interrupted to say that the time was up and asked Maria whether she had any closing word to leave with them.

"One last thought: If you need certainty in your lives, find another line of work. Unless Dr. Simpson has changed the reading list, you're reading a lot about uncertainty and ambiguity in organizations. This is a job that screams ambiguity—about when problems will be resolved," she laughed, "even about when they started. You often don't know what the truth is in a situation or when projects can be completed or how much support you'll receive from staff and parents. You'll seldom receive credit for all the things you do, and you'll often be criticized.

"If you can tolerate that, you'll have moments of great exhilaration. It might be watching a student walk across the stage at graduation who is there only because of your help, or the teacher who thanks you for fighting for his program, or the parent who is grateful that you cut through the red tape to make something happen. Those minutes mean a lot."

Maria paused, trying to find a way to explain why, after everything she had experienced, she still loved the job. "I've been lucky. This job'll devour your personal life, but I have an understanding husband and grown children. I've had wonderful mentors like Professor Simpson and my principal to consult and laugh with. But I feel like I'm doing something. I haven't had much impact on instruction in our school, but I have started some things I didn't have a chance to tell you about, and I keep good programs going. Mainly, though, I'm right in the middle of things, and I can influence some very important decisions. More of them are more individual than institutional, but they're important.

"Last, and best of all, I guess, is that I'm never bored. I really look forward to going to school tomorrow—at least most of the time. I never know what's going to happen. But I do know that the odds are that it'll be something I don't expect."

Driving home, Maria thought of all the other things she could have—probably should have—told them. How much she enjoyed interactions with other adults all day. How much she laughed. How much she enjoyed problem solving and talking professional issues and kicking ideas around, even if you only did it at 4:30 in the afternoon and you knew you'd never have the money to enact them. How close she had gotten to some of the other administrators with whom she worked; there's nothing like being under attack together to build friendships—as long as you survive. How good it felt to solve a theft or to help a student get drug counseling. The sense of accomplishment that comes with helping students find ways to talk to their parents again. The pleasure in being able to find the money to send one of the best teachers to a conference or to get him or her recognized by the local Rotary club.

Of course, there was also the twinge of fear at seeing someone 18 or 20 years old in the hallway during class and not knowing why he was there or what he may be carrying. There were also the endless meetings that did not seem to solve anything and the need to listen politely while people who did not have a clue expressed lengthy opinions. There was the lying awake at night, wondering how you were going to handle what you knew was going to be a very ugly confrontation with a parent or, worse, with a teacher the next day. Parents come and go. The teachers stay. Overall, though, as much as she disliked admitting it, it did sometimes feel good to do battle and win.

Then she asked herself the two questions she seemed regularly to ask herself: Would I do it again? Do I want to stay in this job? And, as usual, she answered herself with two other questions: Could I go back to the classroom and be happy? Is there another way to the principalship? She did not have to answer either question tonight. Tonight she just had to go to the Superintendent's Advisory Committee, and then her vacation would start tomorrow.

Impressions of the
Assistant Principalship

All our knowledge has its origins in our perceptions.
Leonardo da Vinci, *The Notebook*

Our purpose in this book is to communicate what it feels like to become a secondary school assistant principal (AP). "Maria Winston" is, of course, a pseudonym, but not a composite personality. We chose to tell her first-year story against the imagined background of a university class to establish a connection with aspiring administrators (who, we suspect, constitute the largest readership of this book). The events and emotions Maria described were, however, neither fictional nor crafted from the selected experiences of others.

Although a composite story composed of anecdotes collected from several new APs might better show the full range of possible first-year experiences, it would not ring true and would violate our goal of giving readers a sense of what it feels like to become a secondary school AP. More important, a composite presentation of first-year experiences could lead to interpretations that would undercut the value of the book: The events described might seem too impossibly overwhelming and wide-ranging to be probable. The value of Maria's story is not that it shows all of the possibilities, and—as disturbing as some of her experiences were—certainly not all of the worst. Her experience is a typical combination of events, and it highlights the interplay of thought and emotion that characterizes the transition from classroom to office. It underscores the unpredictability and intensity of this transition, one that is not "passed through," but *experienced*. A composite description of an AP's first year communicates none of these points.

The new APs' experiences described in the chapters that follow illustrate the personal impact of the transition into administration. We do not represent this work as a comprehensive study of new APs. We present no statistical analysis of the assistant principalship or of the people who hold it. Such research efforts are commendable and valuable, providing important insights into the nature of administration and secondary schools. Indeed, we employed them to interpret the stories contributed by the APs with whom we spoke. The value of this book, instead, lies in the richness of the individual and collective experience contained in the stories. These anecdotes animate some of the hard data available regarding APs, add to our understanding of secondary schools, and offer aspiring administrators an insider's preview of what awaits them in the office.

The best argument for accepting the beginning assistants' stories, though they are self-reported, is found in the nature of their content. Although some of the stories the APs offered—such as how unprepared they were for the intensity of conflict between staff members or the unanticipated number of meetings they had to attend—were clearly not threatening to their self-images, others potentially were. The fact that they also volunteered personally revealing stories demonstrated a willingness to set ego aside, accept vulnerability in themselves, and trust us. Some, for example, confessed to technical inadequacy in meeting the demands of their jobs; others acknowledged criticisms of themselves by colleagues or supervisors or expressed sore disappointment in specific individuals with whom they worked. Some even admitted they were physically afraid in certain situations; others talked about emotional pressures; and a few revealed marital problems they believed stemmed from job pressures. There was no discernible gain for themselves in such revelations.

Because the first year of an AP represents only a small fraction of an administrative career, it seems fair to ask why we would focus on such a narrow slice of professional life. There are three interrelated, fundamentally simple, and, we believe, important reasons .

First, despite the fact that virtually every secondary school in the United States with an enrollment of more than 600 students has at least one AP (Austin & Brown, 1970; Pellicer, Anderson, Keefe, Kelly, & McCleary, 1988; Reed & Himmler, 1985), APs have been comparatively neglected in research. For teachers and students in those schools, the AP or vice principal or associate principal is the administrator of involvement—the person most frequently and readily available, the one turned to when something is needed immediately (Marshall, 1992; Reed & Himmler, 1985).

Why researchers have not more closely examined the assistant principalship and the work lives of APs is open to speculation. It may be because, through the years, the majority of educational research has been done at the elementary level and far fewer elementary than secondary schools have APs. It may be because the reform movement has passed by the position and the people who occupy it. Perhaps the assistant principalship has not attracted many researchers because its nature is hard to grasp. Although fundamental similarity is found among the roles and responsibilities of principals across the range of secondary schools, little consistency is found in what constitutes an assistant principalship (Austin & Brown, 1970; Pellicer et al., 1988).

The duties assigned to APs vary greatly from district to district, school to school, school to school within the same district, and, over time, even within the same school. Some assistants manage an entire "school within a school" and have a comprehensive range of responsibilities; others have more narrowly defined assignments and obligations. Almost always, their duties include student discipline and some combination of other responsibilities: accounting for student attendance, directing student activities or athletics, supervising and evaluating certificated or noncertificated staff, overseeing guidance, planning and implementing staff development, supervising the activities of selected departments or programs, designing the master schedule, coordinating transportation, and managing the plant and facilities. The possibilities are almost endless. Some schools have only one AP, others have several, and job descriptions are further individualized by variations in school size, setting, and location. It seems impossible to create a generic job description that fits the office, other than "assist the principal" (Marshall, 1992; Pellicer et al., 1988).

Perhaps the most likely reason for lack of attention to the assistant principalship is simply that the position is lost in the shadow of the principalship. As the leader of record—the metaphoric captain of the ship, with all that implies, and the visible representative of the school to the community—the principal has been and remains the focus of school leadership, reform, and research consideration.

Whether any or all of these possibilities explain why APs have received less investigative attention than other educators, an undeniable gap remains in the school administration research and practitioner literature. This gap signals more than just a lack of understanding about the position and the people who hold it. It also represents a significant flaw in the knowledge base required for effective preparation of future secondary school administrators and provides the second reason for this book: APs are important not only in the current administration of schools but also in the future of schooling.

Catherine Marshall (1992, p. viii) observes that "the assistant principalship is the beginning of a career socialization process. Principals and superintendents are the outcome of this process." This observation points to the position of the AP as the gateway to administration for most secondary school principals and a high proportion of district superintendents (Marshall, 1992; Pellicer et al., 1988). It is critically important because it constitutes the initial managerial experience of most secondary school administrators. As such, it is worthy of a close look on its own merits.

The beginning year is a defining phase in the process of becoming a career administrator. Studies of personal and professional transition and research in organizational socialization demonstrate that when people undergo job changes, even within the same field, and especially when they move into management, the first year is crucial to what follows. The attitudes they develop and the repertoire of responses they build have substantial influence on later behavior patterns and leadership capabilities (Berlew & Hall, 1966; Buchanan,

1974; Greenfield, 1984; Schein, 1987; Van Maanen & Schein, 1979). This is particularly important for future principals and district executives because their first-year socialization likely will influence whether they become keepers of the status quo, rebels against the system, or real leaders with a sense of role innovation (Schein, 1987).

The third reason for this book rests on the implications of the first two: APs are the largest group in the pool of candidates for principalships. Effective APs are important to both the functioning and future of secondary schools. Research and common sense tell us that one of the keys to professional promotion is outstanding performance in our current positions (Mobley, 1982; Stumpf & London, 1981). Those who would become secondary school principals usually must succeed first as APs. The better prepared newcomers are for the opportunities and challenges they will meet, the sooner they can become effective in their new positions and the better their odds of early and continued success. It is in the best interests of both the school and the beginning administrator that the newcomer be as prepared as possible.

Roald Campbell and his colleagues (Campbell, Fleming, Newell, & Bennion, 1987, pp. 171-172) point out that educational administration preparation programs oscillate between preparing the person and preparing the person for the role. The former emphasizes developing the individual's "intellectual capacities, educational philosophy, and cultural awareness. Knowledge and self-understanding are primary." The latter emphasizes "shaping the individual to fit the role or roles he or she is preparing to assume." The chief purpose of such instruction is to "help the student understand the job and the institution and to acquire the skills necessary to serve the institution and meet the requirements of the position." Preparation programs in educational administration typically embrace both of these dimensions, but the emphasis is given to the person, and the job prepared for is the principalship.

We believe that preparation programs also must present students with a realistic picture of the assistant principalship because this is the role the vast majority of secondary administrators will initially assume and many will never leave. New APs are rarely fully prepared for their jobs. As a result of the lack of research and practitioner attention to the assistant principalship and because of the nature of secondary schools, most newcomers to the office are unaware of the unique and challenging environment that awaits them. After teachers leave their comparatively familiar and predictable settings and enter the AP's office, they are challenged in unexpected ways. The difference between what they expect and what they find surprises all and shocks some: The pace is faster and the scope of the job is greater than they anticipated; they are not trained for their assigned responsibilities; and the personal satisfactions and stresses are not as they expected.

Carl Jung once observed, "We should not pretend to understand the world only by the intellect; we apprehend it just as much by feeling. Therefore the judgment of the intellect is, at best, only the half of truth, and must, if it be honest, also come to an understanding of its inadequacy" (1923, p. 628). The chapters that follow address the feeling half of becoming an administrator.

Learning the Environment

New Measures of Duty and Time

Now, here, you see, it takes all the running you can do, to keep in the same place. If you want to get somewhere else, you must run at least twice as fast as that.

Lewis Carroll, *Alice in Wonderland*

"Being an assistant principal at this school is just like living in an Indiana Jones movie," he said, leaning forward in his chair. "It seems like I'm into a new adventure every 8 minutes, and I never know what it's going to be." It was late afternoon, and we were talking with a high school AP at his building, asking his impressions of his first year in office. We had planned an hour's visit between 3:30 and 4:30 P.M., but less than 8 minutes into it, he was called out of the office to deal with a problem that had come up during play rehearsal in the auditorium.

Whether they are like Maria, who had a wide background in different educational positions, or are moving into the office directly from the classroom, new APs must immediately come to grips with two new realities. First is the fact that the duties of the office are broader and more numerous than they expected—"The sheer number of things there are to do, including those that don't appear in the official job description," as one man told us. Second, and even more difficult to adjust to, is the fact that the clock runs at a different pace than it did in the classroom. There never seems to be enough time in the AP's day, and what there is flies by so rapidly that it never feels manageable. Most first-year APs simply are not prepared for the time pressures they encounter.

In all of the conversations we had with first-year APs, they remarked on these contrasts between the classroom and the office. The work lives of teachers are measured in fixed periods; they control the type, number, and flow of activities. An AP's work life is one of continuous activity, largely unpredictable in order or scope and frequently dictated by the needs and wants of other people. The volume of demands and the flight of time intersect in such a way that most new APs believe there simply is not time to do all they are called on to do.

The Volume of the Job

Most new APs are surprised to find how much more their new jobs entail than they expected, and the surprise cuts in two directions. First, the tasks they expect to undertake require more of them than they anticipated. "Discipline is what my job description says," one man told us. "It ought to say three quarters of my days and three nights a week." Second, a whole new world is hidden in the phrase "other duties as assigned." New APs find another large portion of work to be done outside their job description.

Adjusting to Expected Duties

Teaching rarely educates classroom instructors to the volume of activities invisibly handled in the office by others every day, and new APs often are caught off guard when they move into the office. As one woman told us:

I didn't realize I had so many things until I got into office and my secretary educated me. She'd say, "Well, this is our department. You're in charge of maintenance, and you're in charge of activities, and you're in charge of, and in charge of, and in

charge of . . ." I didn't realize I had all of those. The surprise
was that all of these people were under my wing, and I was
expected to take care of them.

For most, the scope of the job is more than they had ever imagined:

It was a real surprise! Another whole set of responsibilities
that, as a classroom teacher, I didn't even have a clue about
'cause you don't see the administration a whole lot. And a lot
of the talk as teachers is, "Well, what do those guys do? They're
not that busy. They make too much money." Boy, have my
feelings changed!

It could be tempting to think that the surprise new APs feel about
the number of responsibilities they are asked to assume is somehow
connected to changing schools when they become administrators—
that the assistant's job is somehow bigger in the new school than it
was in the former. But the same feelings of surprise are expressed by
people who become APs in the same buildings where they taught. "I
didn't expect the job to be so comprehensive," one woman said:

It has so many responsibilities. I line up the subs and have
other things to do before my day really even begins. Then it's
discipline, and then a parent in my office, and then a counselor
on the phone, and then something is needed on the grounds.

Even people who previously had jobs that caused them to interact
daily with APs find that they are unaware of the range of responsibilities assistants handle. As one former counselor put it:

I had no concept of what APs were supposed to do. I mean
they were just "the administration," which you tried to avoid.
[laughs] I didn't see them as providing a service, so much as
checking up on us. It's a lot more work than it looks like from
the counseling desk! [laughs] You think you know what the
job is all about, but you don't see the hidden things the AP has
to do.

Among the hidden things that surprise new APs are meetings. "The job description deceives you," one woman said. "A little word like *meetings* means a whole lot more than it ever did in any other job I ever had." Of course, teachers are required to go to faculty meetings and to department, grade level, or teaching team meetings. In-service and staff development meetings periodically take some of their time as well. Depending on their level of involvement, some teachers spend time in curriculum meetings, on task forces, or in union activities. Most of these are held after school. Teachers who become APs discover that they still have to attend not only many of the meetings they had attended as teachers but also countless others both during the workday and beyond it:

> There's an enormous number of meetings: site meetings, leadership council meetings, teacher meetings, district meetings, parent groups, ad hoc committees, student groups, assistant principal and student affairs meetings, athletic league meetings. Just a great many I didn't expect.

As administrators, new APs chair many more meetings than they did as teachers. Even when they are not in charge, they still hold an increased and focused responsibility for committee accomplishment. As one woman observed:

> Then there are the meetings they want me to chair—groups I wasn't even involved in before. Just meetings, meetings, meetings. The worst ones are after a problem or when people won't cooperate on something or when we have a controversy. We used to talk about how periodically we'd have to sit down and have these meetings where we held everybody's hands and got them working together again. But I never really had a concept of what that was all about before I came into this job and how irritating it can be!

Irritation at having to attend numerous meetings is apparently common among administrators. One study found meetings to be their second highest stress-producing activity (after attempts to remain in compliance with all federal, state, and organizational policies and regulations) (Gmelch & Swent, 1984).

Although aspiring APs are exposed in their university credential-ing programs to some of the responsibilities they will be asked to assume, many specific elements of an AP's job often are overlooked in administrative course work. These have to be learned as they are being done. One man put it this way:

> There were a lot of things I didn't even know that I didn't know.

A female counterpart, who had moved into her position from a junior high school teaching position, echoed him:

> It surprised me how much I didn't know, [laughs] especially like the details of attendance office operation and some of the serious discipline stuff. We never dealt with that sort of thing in my ed leadership classes.

Technical parts of the job often surprise new APs because there is much more to them than appears at the surface. Paramount among these are the interactive parts of teacher supervision, the intricacies of master schedule construction, and the pervasiveness of the law, especially in discipline administration.

The challenges of teacher supervision are discussed in Chapter 5, but the surprise of technical complexity in some tasks can be illus-trated here by new AP reactions to building a master schedule. Every first-year AP we talked with who was assigned responsibility for the master schedule during his or her first year found the task more com-plicated than anticipated. One described how difficult it was for him:

> I wasn't prepared for this. We studied schedules a little in one of my credential classes, but we never really built one. I saw some of it when I did my fieldwork, but I was only there part of the time, and I didn't have to live with it like I do now. And when there was a problem, even if I was there, they got on the administrator at that school about it. Now they're all after me: When will it be done? Why does this have to be there? Can't I get it at fourth period? I've always had first period prep. And

on and on. I don't know how to solve those problems. I know
I'll learn, but it's hard, and God, it's slow. I thought schedules
were mechanical, but they're also political!

Constructing a junior high schedule for the first time can be
difficult; constructing a senior high schedule for the first time can be
overwhelming. Because of the varieties of requirements and a wide
range of electives, scheduling a comprehensive high school can be
extremely complex. We talked with a woman coming to a high school
from a junior high, where she had built the master schedule while
working as a counselor and had thought it challenging. In high
school, she found the job to be even more complicated than she had
expected:

> The thing I was least prepared for was the complexity and the
> intricacies of balancing the master program. Building all the
> new classes and how it all inter-works at the high school was
> the hardest thing because at the junior high you don't have
> the variables, and once it's set, it's set for a year. You don't have
> the mass of electives. I didn't have the conflict matrices and
> all of that. I had no idea about how to use those. [laughs] I
> think that was the hardest thing. Having it hit me right off the
> bat: the classes overcrowded, building new sections, offering
> auxiliary assignments, that was all part of it.

One man rather graphically told how he came to grips with it:

> I thought the master schedule would be a lot easier, but now
> I know why they call it the KILLER! I understand the theory
> behind it. It's that last 2% of the master schedule that throws
> fits. What are you going to do? I'm one of those input people:
> Gimme input! Then, finally, you just tell yourself, all right,
> throw up now and decide something.

Master schedules, teacher supervision, and certain elements of
attendance accounting and school budgeting are inherently technically complex, and new APs more or less expect they will have to
struggle with them for a while. The surprise is that the struggle is

more intense and longer lasting than anticipated. Beginning APs often expect other parts of the job to be more easily learned and less complicated in nature. Often, however, even those that are naturally simpler in operation become complex because of legal considerations.

The law reaches into virtually every aspect of an AP's operation. One of the most common things we heard from new APs was that they wished they had had more law education in their preparation programs and that they needed, as one man put it, "legal booster shots" periodically to keep up with the changes in law they needed to know about. One AP spoke for many when he said:

> I was least prepared for all the legal ramifications of things you say or don't say when you're dealing with staff or parents. We're in such a litigious society. You have to be so careful how you phrase something, and you have to cover so many bases. It's so easy to get tripped up in due process and getting strung out, not because you've handled the situation wrongly, but just because you haven't dotted the right "i" in the procedure. And then you end up having to eat your words. That's not very pleasant.

For new APs, discipline administration is usually the place legal concerns surface first and most often. Many new APs dread discipline because they know it involves almost continual confrontation and unpleasantness, but few expect it to be as technically complicated as it is. The complications arise from a combination of human nature and legal constraints. Each is difficult to deal with in itself; mixed, they pose a formidable challenge.

For those who have never dealt with discipline before, the longest and most difficult task is learning school regulations and the law. However, learning the rules, regulations, procedures, and legalisms is not really what drains new APs. The taxing nature of discipline administration is rooted in dealing with human problems in a legal environment. Discipline administration requires intelligence, industry, resourcefulness, and emotional strength—elements discussed in Chapter 4. It suffices here to say that these elements are required because discipline administration is complex and time consuming.

In fact, discipline is the greatest consumer of most assistants' time—the black hole of the office. Research on the work lives of APs indicates that student discipline hogs their duty time, regardless of the size, location, or demographics of the school (Ancell, 1988; Dwywer, 1994; Patton, 1987; Pellicer et al., 1988; Smith, 1984; Staff, 1988). This consumption, of course, negatively impacts their ability to meet other responsibilities and is one of the major reasons for the job's unpredictable and hectic pace.

Several reasons explain why discipline is complicated and requires so much time. First, of course, are the legal considerations. Assistants must proceed cautiously to ensure meeting due process requirements. Considering the high incidence of litigation against schools in the United States, most districts prudently require extensive documentation:

> Then you've had a fight. You can kill your morning or your afternoon because you have to find out what happened and document it with what's called a "referral for immediate action," and it's paperwork six pages long. If you're moving two or three kids out, that's three forms, and you have to go and get the kids' cums [cumulative files] and their test results and their attendance and their grades. It's just a monster that consumes your day.

The process is more complicated if the participant is a special education student:

> I feel hamstrung dealing with special ed students. The law says I can't suspend or expel a student if the infraction was a function of their handicap. Theft or obscenity or disrespect aren't just theft or obscenity or disrespect, they're psychological issues. We have to convene the kid's committee and review the IEP [Individualized Education Program] and what the school psychs say. All the time, the problem is hanging out there.
>
> The worst is when a special ed student is involved with a regular student in something. Then I have to follow two separate procedures in dealing with the incident. Worse even than that, though, is that the consequences can be different. I

get trapped when the regular kid's parent says, "Yes, but why didn't the other kid get the same punishment?"

Time demands and complexity increase if an arrest is involved:

> We caught a kid carrying dope, and it looked like he might be a seller. In this district, possession of drugs gets you arrested. I couldn't believe the paperwork I had to complete on this the first time it happened! Let me tell you, it was amazing. I had to write an incident report for the files, then notes for his cum file and discipline record. Then I had to get written statements from the people who had seen him with the drugs and from the campus monitor who brought him in. Then I had to write the suspension form out and then contact his counselor. Then the principal had to be notified because this was his second offense, and in our district that means a recommendation for expulsion has to go to the superintendent. The principal has to sign and send it, but guess who writes it? Then I had to write the letter home to the parents about the suspension and the recommendation for expulsion. Oh, I forgot. I also had to provide a "possession trail" for the police because we wanted an arrest: The kid had the dope, then the monitor had it, then I had it, then I gave it to officer so-and-so. Do you know how long all that takes?

Discipline administration also consumes time because students are minors, and most incidents cannot be resolved until parental contacts have been made:

> I suspended a student for her part in a theft in the girls' gym locker room but couldn't get ahold of either of her parents. We can't just turn a suspended student loose. We have to legally transfer responsibility to the parents. So here she was, suspended at 10 in the morning but sitting around the office here until almost 2 in the afternoon. For God's sake, we had to bring her lunch!

Hard-to-reach parents are a fact of life for an AP:

I had some trouble contacting parents once in a while when I was a teacher, but I didn't call that many, and when I did, I often called at night, so I caught somebody at home. But in this job, I'm calling someone all the time, and it's hard to get them. Some people don't want to be called at work. Some people work at places that won't put calls through. I have a terrible time getting people to call me back, and then when they do, I'm likely to be out of the office somewhere. Some people will call back on their lunch hour, which is when I'm out on the campus, but many just don't. Maybe they know it's going to be bad news.

A second complicating factor in discipline administration is that most incidents cannot be anticipated even though certain times and conditions signal their likelihood. APs soon learn that fights, smoking, and drug infractions are most likely to occur before school, at breaks, at lunch, and after school, but they are certainly not exclusive to those times. Thefts occur any time, intruders almost always appear unannounced, and there is no way to know when a teacher will decide to send a misbehaving student to the office:

I've been surprised by the frequency of problems. It seems like when it rains, it pours. It isn't like you have any control. One day, two days, you can have a real quiet campus; then the next day, you can have 10 or 12 major incidents. It makes it almost impossible to plan anything.

Discipline requires an immediate response, so it frequently intrudes on other responsibilities, including the resolution of other discipline problems. Discipline creates delays:

When you're right in the middle of doing everything else, there's a fight. You go break up the students, and then you have to work on finding out what the story was and why the fight was going on, and call the parents, and suspend the kids, and so on. Anytime you have something planned is when the day breaks up. I didn't expect that. I'm trying to do a single task, and all these things get in the way.

The third reason discipline is complicated and takes so much time is that APs usually have to deal with situations they did not initiate (Reed & Himmler, 1985). They need to gather information about how an incident began and developed before they can take any kind of action. This task can be difficult when conflicting versions are presented:

> Do you know how long it takes to figure out what really happened? The only clue I ever had about the lying that goes on was when I sent a kid to the office once and he told this whopper about what had gone on in class. Now I hear whoppers all the time! A student will look me right in eye and tell me she didn't say such-and-such, and the teacher will say she did. Those are the easy ones. You'll get all kinds of stories about how and why a fight started. You have to talk to each student separately, and then you have to find and talk to other students you think might have witnessed it, and they might or might not tell you anything. And what they tell you might or might not be the truth; it depends on who they're friends with or who they're afraid of. Try getting a student to tell the truth about a drug deal. And not all the lies are from students. Teachers lie to me, and parents lie to me. It takes a long time, and it's sometimes a real sensitive process to sort it all out.

Finally, discipline gets complicated because teachers who send students to the office expect they will receive a timely report of discipline administered in line with their own definition of justice. This process is complicated when the AP applies other than the expected consequence and the teacher objects to the way the student was handled:

> I learned this real quickly: You can't satisfy everybody, and sometimes it seems like you can't satisfy anybody. A teacher sent a student to me last week for being disrespectful. He had had this kid in class last year and doesn't have much patience with him. Since it was the first offense this year, I gave him a warning, called the parent, and gave him detention, told him and his mother that if it happens again, he'll probably be removed from the class.

I wrote a note to the teacher, telling him what I'd done. He comes storming in here right before lunch, wanting me to take the kid out of his class right now, complaining that I'm way too soft and that I've forgotten what it's like to be in the classroom.

I told him to sit down and close the door and we'd talk about it. I didn't change anything, but it took a half hour of my time, and he's still pissed at me. I don't know what will happen the next time he sends someone to me, but I'm sure he won't be satisfied with what I do.

Sometimes teachers are not that direct. Then the resolution can take even more time and have effects that even may complicate future incident resolution:

I had a teacher who got mad at me because she thought I was too lenient with a student she'd sent, but she never said anything to me directly. But she sure made a point of telling other people about it. I didn't hear about it for a week, until a couple of people told me that [name] was bad-mouthing me in the coffee room. I was really upset. I talked about it with a friend of mine, and she said she thought I absolutely had to confront her. So I went out to her classroom during her preparation hour and told her about this rumor I'd heard that she'd been talking about me and wasn't happy with the way I handled discipline. It was bad. I spent the whole hour with her and didn't resolve anything.

In combination, these factors compound the time-consuming nature of discipline administration. New APs' expectations that problems can be confronted and resolved immediately are eroded by the realities of the process:

I was surprised by how much time discipline takes up; it seems like 80% to 90% of my time. I'd like to be more concerned with staff development. I haven't even had the opportunity to visit classes yet. When I was in the classroom, I thought the most important thing the AP did was disciplining my kids. I was selfish that way. I know there are lots of other important things for APs, but I can't seem to get to them.

Adjusting to Unexpected Duties

Although sitting through meetings, wrestling with discipline, and constructing master schedules are difficult and time consuming, they are, at least, tasks new APs anticipate and for which they have had some preparation. Some duties, however, they are not prepared for, and their unpredictable emergence further broadens and complicates the job. Even those lucky enough to have had realistically focused preparation programs find themselves carrying responsibilities that do not appear in their job descriptions. New APs repeatedly told us they were asked to handle things they had never anticipated. One AP's remarks were typical:

> I'm supposed to be an assistant principal. The word is *principal*. I thought I knew what that meant. I expected to be doing curriculum work and teacher supervision. I had no desire to do discipline, but I knew I'd have to—so I do it. I do all these things. I think I do them pretty well, but I know I could do them a lot better if I didn't have to do all these other things. I didn't know I'd be a computer technician part of the time, or the attendance office clerk when the woman gets sick, or that—for Christ's sake—I'd be the nurse some days. I was told I would supervise the driver-training program, but I didn't think that meant going to pick up cars from the dealer who repairs them—all kinds of stuff I didn't know I'd be doing.

Another woman told us:

> I never wanted to be a counselor, but I am one, and it's nowhere in my job description. And I don't mean just to students. I do a lot of student counseling because of discipline, but I was never prepared for the counseling I do with adults. I'm telling parents how to deal with their kids; I was here 2 hours after school one day with my secretary, who needed someone to talk to because her daughter's pregnant. A lot of this is heavy-duty.

Adjusting to the Time Required by Their Duties

New APs expect that the job will require more time than teaching, but they usually do not realize the impact this load will have on them. Even considering the time teachers spend grading students' papers, administrative days are longer than teaching days, and APs are out at night much more often. But the real difference is not in the number of hours, it is in the nature of them; APs must adjust to hours that are qualitatively different from the ones they used to put into teaching. These are spent supervising students or participating in meetings—responsibilities that require them to be physically, legally, and politically alert, responsive, and responsible. As teachers chaperoning a dance or an athletic event, they could always turn to an administrator in an emergency; now they are the administrators to whom teachers turn. The following comment reflects a common experience:

> The amount of time! I knew there was going to be some time, but I didn't know it was going to be like this. I'm working 6 days a week. I get here at 7:00 [A.M.]. I leave at anywhere between 6:00 and 7:00 [P.M.], if there's not a game. If there is, then I get here at 7:00, leave at 10:00, 10:30, 11:00. And then I come back on Saturday or Sundays for a 2- to 4-hour stint, depending on how many memos I have to do, how much planning for the next week. At some point, I'm going to have to make a decision whether it's worth it or not to do what I'm doing now in terms of the hours I'm putting in, 'cause I'm letting some things slip, but I'm also very infatuated with this job right now.

Even those who have had a preadministrative glimpse of the job from a related position, perhaps as activities or athletic director, sometimes are unprepared for what they find:

> I spent 3 years as an athletic director here. In my book, that's on the edge of an administrative position, so I saw a lot of what administrators do. I wasn't quite as surprised at the amount of time, but I didn't really know the nuts and bolts until I actually got into the job. This week is typical: I've had a meeting

every morning, starting at 7:00 or 7:15, and I've had two meetings in the evening this week also, and supervision of a basketball game. Nobody ever knows the time demands until they're in the job.

Isolated in the classroom, many teachers are surprised, when they move to the office, to find that activities at a secondary school campus are nearly continuous, especially in high schools. For those assigned plant management responsibility, the school is effectively "open" 24 hours a day, 365 days a year:

The high school is open from 7:00 in the morning until 10:00 at night. Then it's open on Saturdays, sometimes Sundays. That's a problem for me as one of the administrators in charge of the plant. I thought it was an 8:00 to 4:00 kind of job, but [laughingly] noooooooo.

Another high school AP, who had come from a junior high, confirmed the experience:

It was shell shock, coming in and saying "Who? Me?" [laughs] It was a 16-hour day for the first semester—at least through football season. When you first start a job, especially as new as it was to me coming from junior high, I found that no matter how much time I put in, it wasn't enough. I was spending a lot of time but not understanding a lot of the things.

The impact of these time demands is not limited to an in-school setting. Learning to cope with home-job conflict is a transition task that is both common and difficult (Feldman, 1976a, 1976b, 1981; Louis, 1982). Afterhour activities are a major cause of stress because they cause personal conflicts with friends and family (Gmelch & Swent, 1984):

One of my frustrations is the lack of time with my family. I knew the job took more time, but I didn't expect it to be that much. I only see my [teenage] son now about 2 hours a week.

He works and goes to school. I couldn't—wouldn't—have done it with small children.

It might be tempting to think that this is typically a woman's response, but this comment came from a man. Research reveals that women managers often have greater stress and difficulty in coping with occupational time demands because of their socialization toward home responsibilities (Nicholson & West, 1988; Ortiz & Marshall, 1988). Still, it does not mean that beginning male APs can expect to escape similar tensions, especially those who are married.

Late in his first year, a man heavily burdened by plant management and teacher evaluation responsibilities told us he had had to attend a meeting at the district office that began at 3:00 P.M. and miraculously ended at 4:15. He decided that, just once, just for today, he would not return to school, but go home early. When he arrived, he got out of the car and walked toward the door, only to have his 5-year-old, looking worried, come out to meet him. The child thought his father was sick because he had never come home from work this early before. The AP thought the story sadly revealing.

Becoming an AP and facing all that the job really entails can be an unpleasant surprise for some, especially for those who find it difficult to be flexible. More than one of the APs told us things like this:

Doing student discipline and attendance would be all right, but you have buildings and grounds, and you have [testing] programs, and you have extended days, and multicultural in-services, and SMART liaison, teacher evaluation. Like I say, if you could just do your job, it would be okay, but they throw in all these other things. So much to do and not enough time to do it.

Whether it is night activities or meetings, discipline or plant management, struggling with new regulations or new relationships, trying to create a master schedule or finding the time to make teacher supervision effective, the last line of this assistant's comment generally sums up the feelings of first-year APs: So much to do and not enough time to do it.

The Pace of the Job

Even more than having too much to do, new APs are stunned by the pace of the job, compared with that of their teaching experience. Three factors contribute to the relentless pace: (a) sharing job responsibilities, (b) coping with unanticipated events, and (c) having to respond quickly to things someone else has begun. In combination, they create "decision-press" situations (Peterson, 1977-1978), which require administrators to change modes of operation, adjust methods of analysis, and shift levels of language complexity, depending on whether they are dealing with students, educators, or community members, all in a limited time period, while deciding which course of action to take. As one AP described the pace:

> I expected it to be exciting, but one adventure after another? It's something that I didn't expect! You know, each day, maybe two or three a week. When it comes to two or three a day, unceasing! I'm thinking all the time: Hey, you know, I thought that last one was a humdinger, but what am I getting myself into now? Really, that's what it is. I think it's the frequency of the activities.

The confidence APs have in the time-management techniques they learned in university classes, workshops, or staff development programs is washed away by the flood of demands:

> I used to make up my little "to-do" list and come to work. Then, 10 things would happen before I could get to the second thing on my list—sometimes before I could get to the first. Now I only make up my list when I work on days when there aren't going to be any students here.

Teachers, counselors, and activity directors find it possible, most of the time, to plan lessons, appointments, or projects—an ability that evaporates in the move to the office. A new AP for discipline and athletics described it this way:

It's the type of job that you really can't plan for. It's one that's almost reactive. I'm normally very organized, and that in itself has been the biggest adjustment for me. There are days when I plan a list of things to do and never get to the first thing on it because of the surprises and the unexpected activities. There should be opportunities for me to have a chance to come up for air, but I have days with absolutely no rest periods. And sometimes it seems as though those days stretch into weeks. It's just a new experience to have so many disruptions.

The pace of the job is driven by the fact that most problems require immediate responses. "You just have to move! And nobody showed me that in any training program," a new AP told us. Another assistant said it well:

You're always worried that if you miss something, it will come back to haunt you. I always felt like I had things under control before, could plan for them—not now. You can't turn your back on something, 'cause that might be *the* thing!

The seemingly unstoppable flow of unpredictable and immediately demanding tasks makes it difficult for most first-year APs to accomplish the goals that originally drew them into administration:

My goal was to be in the classroom helping teachers and to be informally evaluating them and helping them with their problems in the curriculum, but I never get out there as much as I'd like. I had hoped that, in the first couple of months, before things started rolling, I would be able to get out and meet individually most of the teachers on the staff and be in their classrooms, and that just didn't happen. And then, well, actually, the day after school opened, we had 150 more kids show up than we expected, and we had to build classes and re-do the master program that had been built by my predecessor. And I was just coming in fresh. So I didn't get to be out there [laughs] as I'd hoped.

Shulman (1989) has observed that time tyrannizes teaching. If that is true, the time and pace demands of the AP's office absolutely dominate and sometimes terrorize new APs. But despite all of these challenges, we were surprised to learn how many enjoy, even revel in, the fast pace. A guidance office AP was typical when she told us, "I guess I just get the feeling that this is really a niche, my niche. It makes use of all my interests and my strong points." An AP for discipline echoed her feeling:

The pace of the job was a tremendous surprise, 100%. My dad never really commented too much about anything, but when he found out what my job is like, he said he'd really like to see me go to veterinary school and stop this racing-around nonsense. But I don't want to. I love it. It's interesting.

Perhaps one AP summed it up when he said, "This is the goddamnedest roller coaster ride! I'm pulled in every direction at once, and they all want it yesterday. It's great."

Reshaping Perspectives
Administering Discipline

A few strong instincts and a few plain rules.
Wordsworth

"**B**eing responsible for discipline has really changed my attitude."
The young AP gazed reflectively out the window at a lone
skateboarder negotiating a sidewalk curb. "I always thought that if
they're well behaved in my classroom, they'd be well behaved out
on the campus. Well, guess again!" He threw his hands up in mock
surprise. "I never had any real problems, but others sure do. It took
a while to really sink in that the 1,800 kids in this building have
different ethnic, social, and economic backgrounds and *lots* of differences of opinion. I had no clue about what maintaining . . . [here he
made quotation marks with his fingers] 'a safe environment' really
includes. No clue."

He echoed a theme axiomatic in our conversations with new APs:
Discipline administration is full of surprises. Of all the duties assumed by new APs, the administration of discipline most sharply
separates their expectations from reality and reshapes their perspectives on students, teachers, parents, and themselves. In university
classrooms and educational literature, discipline receives less attention than other administrative duties and values; but when discussion

stops and the job begins, APs find that managing student behavior commands their time and attention. The demands of organizational stability establish discipline as a priority over instructional leadership (Mitchell & Spady, 1977; Reed & Himmler, 1985).

Not every new secondary school AP has official responsibility for discipline, but virtually all engage in it sooner or later. In fact, over 90% of APs in the United States are assigned some formal responsibility for maintaining discipline (Austin & Brown, 1970; Pellicer et al., 1988). The rest, like all educators, are bound by law to take some sort of action whenever they become aware of illegal or dangerous student behavior. Between the daily flow of events in the school and the array of activities that APs supervise outside of school hours, becoming involved in discipline is a matter of time, not chance.

Student Control and Job Identity

APs are associated almost invariably with discipline. The stories the new assistants told us showed responsibility for discipline so deeply ingrained in the AP identity that those who do not visibly assume at least a minimum level of accountability for it, whether formally assigned or not, may be resented by other assistants. Discipline administration functions as a proving ground that tests administrators because its pace and dynamics are unpredictable. Incidents hold the potential for intellectual, philosophical, legal, emotional, and even physical confrontation—not only with students, but also with parents, teachers, counselors, and other administrators. Managing all of this becomes a measure of a new assistant's ability and judgment—even character. Discipline is also the most demanding of responsibilities (Austin & Brown, 1970; Brown, 1985; Carona, 1986; Marshall, 1992; Pellicer et al., 1988; Reed & Himmler, 1985; Smith, 1984; Stoner & Voorhies, 1981). On paper, it seems to be only one of many responsibilities, but as illustrated in Chapter 3, the time requirements of discipline administration are enough to frustrate an AP's best efforts to give priority to instructional matters. Without support and participation from other administrators, the psychic costs to the AP can be tremendous. Other APs who do not help with discipline appear to enjoy position and compensation without having to endure their fair share of conflict, sacrifice, and risk.

Discipline receives priority attention in schools because faculty and staff members demonstrate a preoccupation with student deportment (Moles, 1990; Rafilides & Hoy, 1971; J. M. Williams, 1979; M. Williams, 1972; Willower, Eidell, & Hoy, 1967, 1973; Willower & Jones, 1963). Teachers perceive students' breaches of discipline as serious threats that go beyond interfering with their ability to do their jobs. Teachers report that discipline problems are sources of professional and personal stress, even fear, and shadow their public image (Baker, 1985; Bauer, 1985; Center for Education Statistics, 1987; Curwin & Mendler, 1988; Metropolitan Life, 1986). A significant number, in fact, consider leaving the profession because of discipline problems (Center for Education Statistics, 1987).

Carlson (1964) advances an interesting theory about why these concerns obsess educators. He believes that educational institutions share at least one characteristic with prisons and mental institutions: Staff members and "clients" do not pursue common goals because the clients are there by law, rather than by choice. The staff engages in activities aimed mostly at changing client behavior, and students, like prisoners or patients, are required to accept the services. But some students actively resist being changed. This resistance establishes an atmosphere of tension and potential conflict, made worse by the fact that these activities all take place within an organizational context designed to minimize student ability to resist.

When planning lessons, teachers are concerned both with the quality of instruction and with class control. They incorporate ideas, activities, and transition mechanisms with a deliberate intent to capture student attention, overcome their resistance to new ideas, and secure their cooperation (Clark & Peterson, 1986; Corwin & Borman, 1988; Doyle, 1986). This motive may explain, in part, the enduring tradition of the lecture method, which leaves the teacher in complete control of the flow of the class, allowing the lecturer to simplify and telescope complex topics for skeptical, impatient students (McNeil, 1988).

Teaching involves continuous monitoring of student behavior, in addition to ongoing assessment of student learning. By observing student reactions to the pace, rhythm, and duration of activities, teachers ascertain the level of student engagement and susceptibility to distraction. Without this monitoring, teachers fear that the educational activity will dissolve into chaos (Emmer, 1981, 1984; Emmer & Evertson, 1981; Kounin, 1970; Yinger, 1979). Understandably, then, teachers want discipline problems handled immediately and in ways that reinforce their classroom control.

Teacher-student conflict is not the only concern. Teachers also must become involved in student-student conflict because adults are legally responsible for student safety and welfare. Schools are expected to teach appropriate interpersonal skills, and when students and staff members disagree about what is appropriate, the adult expectations and directives must prevail.

Because of differences in their philosophies, personalities, and educational goals, staff members may disagree among themselves about how best to prevent and resolve conflicts. Evidence suggests that as teachers grow in experience, they gradually give up the idea that there is one best way to deal with conflicts, and they come to believe that situations call for varying responses (Weick & McDaniel, 1989). Attitudes toward discipline are influenced by experience, gender, and cultural backgrounds. Because of differences in training and responsibilities, counselors and administrators sometimes differ sharply over how best to resolve discipline problems (Eidell, 1965; Hoy, 1965; Mitchell & Spady, 1977; Sue & Sue, 1990). Folding in the varying perspectives of teachers, it becomes clear that the chance of getting universal agreement on either standards of student behavior or appropriate methods of enforcement is more a hope than a reality. Because of lack of agreement, disputes are appealed to authority, and APs are put in the position of having to negotiate the resolution of individual conflicts.

Redefining Relationships With Students

Discipline forces new APs to develop new relationships with students. In the classroom, students were dealt with individually as the targets of instruction; in the AP's office, they are more often targets of control and counseling. New APs often expect that students will regard them negatively. The assistant's image is that of the campus "heavy," and many anticipate a loss of the popularity and comfortable relationships they formerly held with youngsters. That sometimes happens, but it is not inevitable, as one AP told us:

> Yeah, I'm sure there are kids who perceive me as a bad guy, but there are a lot of kids on campus who don't. At first, I thought that I would go directly from being the good guy—the activities director that everyone loves—to being the AP everyone hates. And that's not the case. I still feel like there's a lot of kids out there that I can joke around with and tease with and have a good time.

APs can maintain positive relations with the majority of students in the school if they are willing to work at it by mixing in with them in the hallways and at lunch, taking time to talk with them informally at activities, and going out of their way to praise and support students who have gotten into trouble and then straightened out. The most effective APs use all of the resources at their disposal for what one man called "preemptive interventions."

Many students go to an AP for counseling at least as much as they go to their counselors, especially for things of a personal nature, and many APs find that gratifying:

> I had one boy this year who wanted me to go with him to tell his father that his girlfriend was pregnant. I thought, "Now that's a good way to get killed." But the point is that the boy came to me to talk about it. I had given him grief a couple of times when he was sent to the office for mouthing off in class, and once I just exploded all over him. Then we'd joke in the halls. I'd see him and ask him if he'd been sick. He'd say no, and then I'd say that I hadn't seen him in the office for a few days. We'd laugh, but those exchanges were good, and he'd come around and just talk once in a while. Then, when he came in one day to talk about this, it just sort of came out that he appreciated my interest in him. He'd never put it in those words, but that's what it amounted to. I thought I had lost that kind of association when I left the classroom.

Discipline counseling shows new APs a student world often hidden from them as teachers:

> I had no idea of the problem homes of these kids. I think elementary teachers get a better picture, but the high school teacher just has them for 50 minutes, and then they go out and you might never know if there's a death in the family, if they come from an alcoholic family, what kind of abuse they've had. And in the AP's office, it's brought up all the time and comes from all different directions: from counselors, attendance, discipline, special ed; I get to hear a lot from that. So that was kind of a shocker.
>
> There are so many kids who need help of one kind or another, and I don't know how to give it to them. I really think APs need to be trained as counselors. I want to help, but it's hard to know what to do. You can't be sure what you're doing is legal, and you can't take kids home. I wasn't ready for this.

Once aware, however, new APs frequently try to intervene in students' lives. Many spend a great deal of time counseling students and try to find professional counselors or agencies to help. A common disappointment for new APs is that they do not know whether their efforts have helped. It is rare to see a student turn around in only 1 year, so new APs have to take it on faith that they have produced a positive effect:

> I don't know if I'm doing that much good. [An experienced AP] tells me that I can make a real difference in a student's life, but it's hard for me to see it. He tells me stories about how some seniors I know were hellions 3 years ago and headed for disaster, but he and some of the others around here got ahold of them and straightened them out. But he also tells me about some kids who you just have to wash your hands of because they'll just drain you and never change a bit. But his favorite story is always about [a boy] whom he pressured to stay in school and get his diploma and then join the service. He talks about how he came back the first time in his uniform. Just a

neat kid. And [the experienced AP] knows it never would have happened if he hadn't "adopted" the boy.

One AP observed how the whole thing seemed to have evolved for her during the first 7 months of the year:

> I guess one surprise is that I like working with discipline. It's my contact with students. And if I can treat them with dignity, they're pretty responsive. I saw maybe 40 or 50 kids today, and I had one who got a little profane, but that's a pretty good batting average right there. I don't win all the arguments, and I don't always convince them, but consequences can be dished out to kids in a way where they may not be happy about it, but they know they're not treated badly. Most of these kids say "thank you" on the way out! I guess I've built kind of a reputation for being tough and for being fair. One of the teachers said he had a rowdy fourth period and all he had to do was threaten to send them to me. [laughs] I think that the kid who has a problem will come and see me and the kid who is a problem will be concerned about it.

Reshaping Perspectives on Parents and Teachers

The administration of discipline also causes new APs to see parents and teachers differently. As APs, they have different reasons for interactions with teachers and parents from those they had when they were teachers themselves, and changes in the reasons for engagement bring changes in the relationships.

Parents

Discipline administration opens a new dimension in dealing with parents, and the relationship is often tense. The tension is a major stressor of secondary school administrators (Gmelch & Swent, 1984). Teachers interact with most parents because parent-teacher conferences are scheduled routinely. In such settings, the teacher's report of student progress and attitude is often very positive, and the conference is a rewarding experience. On other occasions, teachers contact parents to enlist help in improving the student's academic performance or attendance because they are concerned about something in the student's personality or demeanor that suggests a need for counseling or because of a troubling behavior pattern. Once in a while, teachers contact parents to praise a student's improvement in behavior or achievement. In most cases, even though an initial tension may arise between teachers and parents, the mind-set is one of cooperation, and the outcome is usually predictable.

APs, however, rarely call with good news. Just the knowledge that the AP is calling is enough to raise a parent's anxiety level because the trouble in secondary schools can be very serious. One of the most difficult things new APs must adjust to is the unpredictability of parental response to negative information about their youngsters:

> I wasn't prepared for the way some parents react in a conference situation. See, most all the parents I dealt with before because I had gifted kids most of the time were real good parents. Even when I had remedial classes, I think the parents were very supportive. Now, as the guy in charge of whether or not you're going to be here at school, I see a lot more criticism. Parents are going to blame everything from the second-grade teacher who screwed up their kid's life to what happened here. I'm the guy they're going to be talking to about all those problems. I wasn't prepared for the amount of negative feedback I've gotten.

Another AP echoed the experience:

> I never quite know what I'm going to get when I call a parent. Sometimes, probably most of the time, I get disappointment and then cooperation and then a promise that they'll talk with their child. Other times, they'll blame it on the teacher, who they'll say is unreasonable, or they'll say that it's the other student's fault—that happens a lot with fights—or they'll want every little detail and accuse me of being unfair if I can't provide it.

But the more serious the infraction, the more likely that I'm going to have a problem with the parent. Not all the time, but enough. Then, sometimes, I get taken completely by surprise. I had a boy brought in first semester in possession of marijuana. He said it wasn't his. You hear *that* all the time. I asked him whose it was, and he wouldn't tell me. I told him that I had him and I had the pot and that they were going to jail together if he didn't cooperate and tell me whose it was. Finally, after almost an hour, he broke down and said he would tell me. I said, "Okay, who?" He said, "It's my mother's."

I couldn't believe it. I was just livid. So I told him: "That's it. You just keep lying. See what it gets you. I'm calling your mother right now." So I called Mom, explained the situation, and then said, "And now he's telling me the stuff is yours." There was a moment of silence, and then she said, "Well, it could be. I haven't been able to find everything lately." I almost fell over.

Sometimes parental behavior is passive but still surprisingly nonsupportive. "Some parents talk a good story," one AP told us, laughing. "That's not negative, is it? They say, 'Oh, yes, I really appreciate all you're doing,' then turn around and let the kid completely loose to do whatever he wants!"

Meeting with parents in the office is also something that new APs find disconcerting the first few times. It is one thing to talk with a parent on the phone and quite another to have a full-blown conflict erupt in your office. Sometimes the anticipation is worse than the reality:

We caught a kid with a box of bullets. I suspended him, of course, and called the parent. A little while later, suddenly, I've got his dad at the door. Well, I was really scared of what the father was like if his kid—this gang kid, who has a full box of shotgun shells—I thought, "Oh, no." It turned out the father was not at all what I expected—I mean, a regular old normal person in a suit.

Keep in mind that it's a people job, and you have to be careful not to make assumptions and not to stereotype and to think that because the kid carries a gun that Dad carries a gun.

Or that because the kid got caught drinking that Mom and Dad are total alcoholics. Just try to keep things in perspective and get what parent support you can.

At other times, the negative reality exceeds all expectations:

I thought I could use all my skills, get both mothers in to talk to me about it, and settle this long-term problem between these two boys. I couldn't believe what happened! The struggle between the boys was nothing compared to the struggle between the mothers. The argument went all the way back to elementary school, and they were as much into it, you know, as the kids were, more, in fact. They got so mad when we tried to figure out why this had kept going on that they blamed each other and started yelling and then before I knew it, *they* were fighting. Can you believe it? Two *mothers* slugging it out at the school. I about decided I was in the wrong job right then.

It is also often difficult for new APs to adjust to parental denial. For discipline other than teacher referrals, it is not uncommon for APs to have directly observed the misbehavior, and they find it difficult to maintain a professional detachment when their own eyewitness accounts are challenged:

The surprise comes in the fact that it's hard for me to understand parents who are always in a state of denial: "Yes, my son did it, but . . ." or "No, you caught him, but he didn't do it" attitude. We had a situation that involved some students we caught with alcohol off campus on Senior Ditch Day. Parents questioned what we really saw and were upset that we even went to the park and brought them back to the campus to discipline them. We tried to explain that it was simply an extension of our jurisdiction during the school day. They were willing to fight this all the way to the school board, rather than have their sons and daughters suspended. That was a real surprise. I thought parents would be more willing to accept the fact that their son or daughter had made a mistake and be more willing to work with us, rather than becoming antagonistic and trying to support them in a negative sense.

Sometimes denial protects parents from things they do not want or are not really able to face. New APs sometimes find this difficult to accept:

> We had a gang-related killing in a park south of here. The kid went to this school and was involved in gangs. After he was shot, his mother completely denied his involvement. "He wasn't in a gang. He was a good boy, home every night. He never did this stuff." Well, those of us who worked with him and saw him, and even his friends admitted it, we knew. The mother rejected reality, had no concept of what he was up to. That was really disturbing.

An AP offered his view of why discipline interactions with parents can be difficult:

> The parents feel like they have their own lives now. Their children are big, they're in high school, and it's, "Don't bother me with that. I'm busy doing my own work."

Some APs credit the difficulty they have in working with parents to school demographics, attributing the problems, as one said, to "single, low socioeconomic, non-English-speaking parents who work until 6:00 P.M. and are not interested in school." But other new APs from affluent schools told us they face the same problems. One AP summed it up when he said that the assistant principalship was "a window on society":

> It's the number of parents who have given up: "I can't make her go to school. I can't make her do anything." They throw up their hands. They've lost control at a young age, and as the child gets stronger, they overwhelm the parents. I'm seeing it every day in their relationships, and I didn't see it when I was in the classroom.

I'm beginning to see in this community, which is basically families, dysfunctional families—a lot of them. I mean it's across the board ethnicity-wise, socioeconomic-wise. I mean middle America's falling apart.

Of course, APs are human. They will make mistakes, especially when they are new on the job. Sometimes, in what appear to be airtight cases, things are not what they seem, and the parents are understandably upset:

> During lunch, we had two kids under a sheet in a car, and the campus supervisor went over and tried to get them to come out. Took a little time. The sheet was moving, you know, in a suggestive fashion. So they called me to come to the parking lot. Finally they came out from under the sheet. The boy is kinda fixing his pants, and both kids, especially the girl, were extremely belligerent: "We haven't been doing anything. How come you're not out busting drug dealers?" And this and that. How do we deal with that? I mean, with some dignity.
>
> They refused to come to the office. A couple more administrators came out, and a male AP took the boy, and I took the girl. We got them to calm down and to realize we were treating them fairly. We gave them a short suspension—for disruption and defiance of authority, not for sexual activity—and then had to call the parents.
>
> When I called the girl's father, he really took off on me, telling me his daughter was a straight A student who was a pillar in the church youth group and wouldn't do anything like that, ever! He became abusive with me. When I tried to defend what we were doing, he hung up, yelling that he was going to call the superintendent. I was so mad! Then, when I gave the girl the referral slip, she told me that I had her middle name wrong. That's how I found out I had called the wrong parent—somebody else's father!
>
> I didn't know what to do. Before I could do anything, the phone rang. It was the superintendent. He asked me what was going on out here. I explained my mistake, and he nearly got hysterical with laughter. When he could catch his breath, he

said he was sure I could take care of it myself. Then I had to call the wrong dad back and eat crow. He wasn't very gracious about it either.

I was surprised. The parents, the real ones, were all right— when I finally got the right one. The girl's actual father said, "Well, I know the boy, and he seems like a nice young man." And the dad knew exactly how his daughter was. He said, "I bet she said . . ." and he just went through exactly what she had said just like he'd been there. He was very supportive. So were the boy's parents. I finally got an apology from the young man.

Virtually every new AP is surprised by the unpredictability and intensity of parental reactions, but not all are equally surprised. New APs who have had previous experience in positions that put them in greater contact with parents probably make the adjustment more easily than those who come into the office straight from the classroom. Activities directors, for example, have more contact with parents than do classroom teachers, and although the students they deal with are usually high achievers from supportive families, their parents can be very assertive at times. Counselors have a wide range of exposure to parental behavior. Having worked with parents to improve a student's behavior and attendance and having planned out programs and handled requests for teacher changes, they have fewer surprises when they assume an assistantship.

Experience as a dean all but removes the discipline surprise element for a new AP. Before they become administrators, deans deal with parents through discipline contacts and are exposed to the range of unpredictable behaviors. Some adjustment is still to be made, however. Deans usually are directed, or at least have the opportunity, to refer difficult or very serious discipline cases to the AP. The assistant is stuck with them.

Teachers

Discipline administration also presents role conflict challenges that can initiate a change in a new AP's perspective on teachers. Simultaneously charged with maintaining order and being student advocates, APs are supposed to administer justice and back teachers.

These actions are most often identical, but not always, and each side in a conflict expects full support. These role conflicts in discipline administration strike deep into things that are important to educators. Trying to administer justice and support a teacher whose actions are indefensible can put an AP in an impossible situation:

> You get someone who takes what should have been easy to handle and makes it so the parent has to defend the kid. One of our biology teachers took a squirt gun away from a Hispanic girl. She was flashing it around during class. She had it for some dumb drill team thing at lunch, so she didn't want to give it up when he asked for it. He took it. She said something under her breath, he doesn't even know what, and he turned around and squirted her. She called him a bastard, and he shot right back with *puta*, which is "whore" in Spanish. I can't believe how unprofessional and how unnecessary the whole thing was. This happened yesterday, and now I have a conference with the teacher and the girl and her parents and the principal in the morning.

If unresolved in large numbers, conflicts like these can cause new administrators to question their career choices:

> There was a student who "threatened" a teacher by saying, "This isn't over yet." Well, in dealing with the student and dealing with the teacher, I think the teacher could have stopped the situation before it got to that point. In our district, a threat to a teacher automatically gets a student referred to a committee for possibility of expulsion.
>
> When I pulled the student's records, he's a pretty neat kid who lost his mother last year. He was rushing into school and took a faculty space in the parking lot, and the teacher saw him. The day before, the teacher had sent him out of class for talking. Instead of going up to the kid and saying, "Hey, you shouldn't park in those spaces until 7:50," the teacher came to me, demanding that I do something about it.
>
> So I called the student in, and the student said, "How did you find out about this?" I said a staff member had told me.

He asked who, and I said I couldn't remember, which was a lie; I knew who it was, and so did he. The kid went into the class and said to the teacher, "Why are you after me?" The teacher said something back, and the kid said, "Well, this isn't over yet" and walked away.

I just felt awful about it. I did what I had to do, 'cause that's what the rule said, and my number one responsibility is to support the teacher. The kids graduate, but the teachers are there, year after year. This all surprised me because, I guess from my own background, that never would have happened. In 10 years of teaching, I think I wrote two referrals. It surprised me that a man would allow this to get to such a point. I never thought I'd have to be doing something like this.

Reshaping Perspectives on Discipline Administration

Although discipline administration causes new APs to reshape their perspectives on some characteristics of students, parents, and teachers, its greatest impact is probably on themselves and their perspectives on the nature of discipline. Almost every teacher sooner or later has a confrontation with a student. APs are involved with such encounters all the time, and they cover a wider range of conflicts than most classroom teachers ever know about, let alone encounter. Most play out as relatively calm events, but some are public, loud, and potentially serious. For beginning APs, the frequency and intensity of such incidents can be unsettling and can have a cumulative effect over time.

The bulk of discipline administration is given over to handling the kinds of events teachers and outsiders usually associate with schools. But students are referred to the office for any number of reasons, from the silly to the serious. A high school AP told us:

I get students in here for more things than you can imagine. My first day, I had a 10th-grade girl who had hit a 9th-grade boy because he'd jammed her locker lock with peanut butter and bubble gum. She was twice his size and really punched him. He said he'd done it because she dropped books on his head on purpose whenever they were both there getting the things they needed between classes.

A middle school AP puzzled over how to handle the following incident:

> Four seventh-grade boys decided to make some girls who were bugging them sick. They took a table next to the girls in the cafeteria and sat down to eat as usual. A few minutes later, one of them began to complain that he felt sick. His friends just hooted and made fun of him. He had his back to the girls' table so they couldn't see his face. All at once, he stood up, made a gagging noise, and appeared to vomit all over the table. What the girls couldn't see, since his back was turned, was that when he made the gagging sound, he was holding a thermos of chicken-vegetable soup against his chest, and that's what he spilled all over. The girls were grossed out, but that's not the best part. The best part is that his three friends all started cheering, yelling, "Oh, yeah! Great!" and then took their spoons and started to scoop it up and eat it. A couple of the girls started screaming and ran out of the cafeteria; a couple of others thought they were going to get sick themselves. The worst part was that the teacher on duty there was taken in just like the girls. She was just dumbfounded.

Now what am I supposed to do about that?

Sometimes *students* refer the *teachers* to the AP:

> We have two lovebirds who just can't keep their hands off each other. Every day at lunch, they'd go down to the patio outside the home economics rooms and make out. After a while, they got horizontal on the picnic tables. The home ec teacher eats her lunch in that room with some other teachers, and they could see this out the window. She asked them to cool it, but they were at it again the next day. She warned them to stop or she'd have to do something, but they came back again on Friday.

　　　I guess she just lost it—her patience, I mean. They were stretched out embracing on the table, and she took a roasting pan full of water and threw it on them. They jumped up, all sputtering and mad. She told them that she figured if they were going to act like a couple of dogs in heat, she'd have to separate them like they did dogs.

　　　The two came over here just furious to report what Mrs. [name] had done. I could hardly keep a straight face. I told them they were absolutely right and I should call their parents right away to let them know what had happened and that I'd be reprimanding Mrs. [name]. Well, they didn't want that. They decided they could maybe forgive her and just go to the gym where they had some dry clothes. I haven't seen them again, but I also understand they're not having lunch in the home ec patio.

Although events like these consume an AP's time, they help newcomers keep things in perspective and maintain a sense of humor. The retelling of these stories also helps build camaraderie among administrators. New APs need this because the next level of discipline problem is more serious. Students smoke behind the gym or in the rest rooms or in the parking lot, steal from lockers or classrooms, vandalize school property, and fight:

　　　I was surprised that the worst fights are often between girls. They really mean to hurt each other, and they won't let it go when it's over. I mean, we break it up and suspend both of them, but they'll be at it again before very long, and they'll bring their friends in.

Some fights are just the start of things.

　　　I'll tell you the kind of mess a fight can produce. The day before yesterday, the senior class president got into a fight with one of our real jerks out in the parking lot after commencement practice. I had to suspend both, and our rule is that serious discipline infractions during the last weeks of school take you out of commencement. All hell broke loose. The parents [of the class president] went to the principal, who backed me—thank God—and then went on to the superintendent. He wouldn't give in; now they've talked to an attorney and gone to the board. If we let one of them march, we'll have to let the other one. Graduation is tomorrow night. Everybody is talking to attorneys. I'm waiting for instructions.

In addition to the real fights are other surreal challenges that can take up just as much time and energy:

I was pulled out of a meeting by my secretary, who said that a distraught parent *had* to talk to an administrator and I was the only one here. The mother said her daughter had been punched in the eye when she stepped in front of a boy during a fight. The girl didn't report it because she was afraid of the "bully" who hit her. By this time, school was out, so I couldn't do much investigating, but I took all the information, told her to take the girl to a doctor if the eye looked bad—and it did—and save the bill to present to the perp when we found him.

The next morning, I talked to the principal, the other APs, some students, and the girl's counselor. No one knew anything about a fight, but this girl had provided a detailed description of her attacker. We called in the girl and her parents, and she finally admitted that she'd made up the entire story! She had deliberately hit herself in the eye with a baseball bat, then concocted the story to get attention. So we changed the appointment from an internist to a shrink and sent them on their way.

APs also deal with issues that emerge at school dances, plays, athletic events, and other activities. Intruders, intoxicated students, disruptions, sexual incidents, are all, as one phrased it, "part of the rich tapestry of an AP's life."

I hadn't been to a prom since I was in high school myself. I didn't think I was innocent then—for God's sakes, that was the '70s—but I sure was by '90s standards. We had kids with cocaine this year and groping in the corner that was pretty hot. Nobody ever told me it was part of my "professional duty" to go into a hotel rest room and help a girl because she's had too much to drink and have her throw up all over me. Or that I'd get into a serious debate with someone over a parent's right to serve beer or wine at a pre-prom dinner at their home and then send the kids along to the dance. It's madness. One mother told the principal and me that of course she'd give them alcohol at her home. They were going to drink anyway and that if she didn't allow it in her home, they'd be doing it in a parking lot somewhere. I almost choked when the principal asked her if she loaned them her bed too!

All the problems that beset APs do not have their origins in the school:

A senior here came to school with a punker friend of his to find four guys they said raped [the senior's] sister at a party the night before. These two guys were big, and the four guys they were looking for were all smaller: three sophomores and a junior. Well, they found them at a snack break, and all at once this huge fight is shaping up. I was a distance away when I got a call on my radio that there was a problem in the cafeteria area.

We got over there and grabbed these guys and got them separated and all into different offices. We called the police to arrest the senior's friend as an intruder. Then we tried to figure out what was going on. When the senior said his sister had been raped, we asked the police to stay.

Well, it turned out the girl hadn't been raped at all. This kid's awful herself. The three sophomores and the junior, after denying for a half hour that they had any idea why [the senior] should be after them, finally admitted that they had had sex with her at the party, but they swore it wasn't forced. It was her idea, they said. She was drinking and took a dare from one of her girlfriends that she could handle a "line-up." We thought the boys were making this up.

Then one of the women APs got the senior's sister and a couple of other girls who the boys said had been at the party out of their classes. The other girls wouldn't tell who made the dare, but after a while they independently corroborated the boys' story. In a few minutes, the female AP got the sister to tell her the truth. She had had intercourse with only one boy because they had only had one condom, but she had had oral sex with the other three.

The twist was that when she was coming in at about 3:00 A.M., she made so much noise she woke her brother up. He took a look at her and asked, "What the fuck happened to you?" She was afraid to tell him the truth, so she made up the story that they had forced her. He punched her for being so dumb and then went into a rage. I don't know where the parents were, but the next morning he came here. Christ, it had nothing to do with school, but all at once it was *my* problem.

To a greater or lesser degree in every school, more serious infractions and crimes occur. Serious problems are often more complicated problems, and they stir conflicting emotions and troubling questions in new APs:

I had one boy last semester who was selling drugs and was taking them himself. It just tore me up. On the one hand, I wanted to kill him for selling the shit and messing up other kids. On the other, he was so messed up himself that I wanted to do everything I could to help him. After he was arrested, his mom and dad came in with him. They had been denying that he had any problem with drugs for so long that when this hit them in the face and was undeniable, they came apart. They confronted him here. Everybody was crying. He was going to be expelled, and he was probably going to go to jail. We were pleading with him to get help, get into counseling and into a drug program. He sat right there where you are and said he loved his drugs more than he loved his parents and he wasn't going to give them up. I didn't know what to do then. I've never seen two more shattered people than his parents.

Sometimes fear competes with a sense of duty:

I was the only administrator in the school. The rest were all at a meeting at the district. A scared-looking boy came to my door and said he had to talk to me for a minute. I had him come in and I closed the door. He told me that [name] in his English class the period before had had a gun in his jacket pocket. He was scared to death and begged me not to tell anyone that he had told me. I promised, thanked him, and sent him on to class. Then I was all alone, and I didn't know what to do. I knew this kid, and I was afraid. I knew I had to do something. I found out where [name] was that period and started toward the class, and then I thought better of it and went back and called the police.

Sometime fear wins, and new APs are surprised to find that discipline administration can be just plain frightening. The feelings they experience, which are terribly different from what they expected, can call the whole notion of professionalism into question:

I've had a wild year, and it's only three quarters over. I've had to take a loaded gun off a student, and I had to evacuate the gym when we got a bomb threat over the phone. Both times, my heart was pounding like crazy, and I'm asking myself, What am I doing in this job? Nobody told me about this. I know about teaching. I don't know about this. But, Jesus, I was scared in both those situations—more in the bomb one, I think, 'cause I couldn't do anything about it. I just had to go in and get those students out.

I got a lot of praise for the way I handled those incidents. When we got all through with the police in the gun deal, I worked with the parents and the police and our Counseling Department, and we got the boy into a program. The parents still call me to let me know how he's doing and to say thanks. We kept it out of the papers. I don't even think most students knew about it. My principal says I'm a real pro. I think I am, but I don't know pro what.

Most new APs begin their careers believing that professionalism in education is defined by their ability to affect curriculum and instruction. Too often they find that job success really is defined by their ability to manage student behavior by developing skills in crime prevention, investigation, interrogation, counseling, and security:

> Friday before vacation, we got a call that there was going to be a gang problem with Hispanics and Asians at a bus stop after school; they were coming in carloads. And so each of the four APs went to a different bus stop around the area. Mine was about three quarters of a mile away. I was supposed to be a deterrent, but I stood there thinking, What's going to keep them from shooting me because I'm standing here?
>
> There isn't a week that I don't deal with stuff like this. Now our district has given us long yellow jackets that say STAFF on the back, and on the front [Name] Unified School District Security. That's not the professional image I had in mind.

Experience quickly demonstrates that discipline administration is an emotional endeavor. Fear alternates with disappointment, anger with compassion. Occasionally, exhilaration results from having made a positive difference. The problem is that APs, especially new ones, never quite know what the mix will be. Sometimes situations are sad and surprising:

> I had a parent conference—Samoan kid—to talk about his class cuts and attendance. It was very emotional. The father cried through most of it; the mother cried and left. Finally, the outcome was that I should be dealing with the probation officer because the parents felt they really had no control of the kid. I didn't have any of this information going in, and the father says, "You know he's been shot twice, and we've had to have him in three different schools, and we've moved a lot, and . . ." I'm sitting there, saying to myself, Okay, now don't overreact. Shot. Twice? Gasp! [laughs]
>
> That really surprised me. I was a cheer advisor, had coached, taught physics, did activities. It was like, Oh, my gosh! They have people like this that go to school. I was really surprised by some of the difficulties they face.

Sometimes situations are just heartbreaking:

> Mrs. [name] sent a freshman up on a discipline referral be-
> cause he refused to participate in the class lesson, which in this
> case was watching the movie *The Elephant Man*. The kid looked
> like a cruel parody of adolescence. He's tall and pathetically
> skinny; he wears thick glasses, suffers from terminal acne, has
> a harelip, wears braces, can't seem to afford a decent haircut,
> and according to his mother, is in basic classes because he has
> ADD [attention deficit disorder]. Last Friday, he was hit by a
> car—hit and run, of course—as he crossed the street, and he
> suffered even more damage to a face almost unbelievably
> ugly. I was the one who had to ask him why he wouldn't watch
> *The Elephant Man*. "Because I look just like him," he said.
>
> You find *that* in any guidebook for vice principals.

Discipline administration also makes many new APs feel isolated
in their jobs. In the classroom, teachers are isolated from other adults,
but they share similar responsibilities with every other teacher. Another teacher is next door, the administration is usually quickly
available, and classrooms are filled with students. APs, however, do
not have corresponding support lines, and privacy concerns require
them to be alone with students or parents or teachers. At any one
time, an AP may be the only person in the school working on a
particular problem. Supervision of hallways, grounds, and activities
often takes them unaccompanied into areas where students are likely
to be engaged in prohibited and hidden activities.

APs have the primary responsibility for dealing with whatever
discipline problems erupt at the school. Sooner or later, they will have
their first serious confrontation alone with a student or students, and
it will carry a strong emotional impact. Such experiences are often
not long in coming. One man who had never previously dealt with
discipline outside the classroom had his initiation the week before
school even opened:

> People told me this is just a great school; no problems here.
> Ha! My first encounter here was when I came in August. There
> was a little dance party for the school band members getting
> ready for the opening home football game the next week
> outside here [points to a patio area outside the office]. Band

members are mostly good kids, and no problems were expected, so I worked the event alone. There was a kid who showed up who weighed about 220 and was about 6'5" who wasn't a band member but wanted in. I'm about 185, 6'2", and I've dealt with some big kids before, but this kid was *big*, and he was upset, and it was a real scary situation.

All at once, he was hitting his head against the wall and yelling. Really crazy. He wasn't on drugs, but he was emotionally disturbed. His girlfriend was here, and he wanted to see her. She'd broken up with him or something. He was really upset, and he wasn't going to be kept out of the dance just because he wasn't a band member. He wouldn't obey me, and he wouldn't go away. I had to call the police to come to this nice school without any problems. The band people assured me this never happened before. I should have known right then that I was in for a very exciting year.

A new sense of individual responsibility—broader than any they have had before and from which they feel no escape—is a major contributor to feelings of isolation for beginning administrators. Not only must they act on reports of improper behavior, but they also must anticipate, deter, and search out such behaviors. New APs know such things at an intellectual level, but the associated feelings cannot really be assessed and internalized until they have been experienced:

> I knew there would be drugs here; I'd probably have a weapon, or something would be brought on campus. But then it actually happened and reality set in. All of a sudden *I'm* here, and now *I* am in control. I think that was the biggest shock.
>
> Before, as a teacher, I could sit back and say, "Hey! Get that guy!" or just be there backing someone else up. Now I'm in a leadership role. I'm in the limelight and can't get out.
>
> I think as time goes by, you learn to like that role and to accept it, but at first, you're looking around and thinking, Is someone else going to take care of this problem? It's an awakening experience when the answer is no.

The experience of isolation can be mediated if the administrators handle discipline as a team:

> We've got a wonderful setup here. I have a friend over at [another] high school, and she's not happy at all with how things are arranged. Their offices are spread out all over the campus. The administration building here is at the front of the school, and we all have our offices in the same cluster. And it's a good thing. We had a student pull a knife on the principal one day. I couldn't believe it; it was like something out of a movie. But we were all right here, and we had him subdued in a minute, and someone knew to call the police. I like knowing I'm not alone if there's a problem here.

If others are not close by, as with this assistant's friend, the situation can be very different:

> This is a big campus, nearly 50 acres, and we've tried to cover it by stationing administrators all around it. The only problem is that if there's a problem somewhere that takes more than one person to handle, it can seem like a long time before anyone gets there. I had a custodian call me just before the holidays one day and tell me that there were kids coming across our practice field and he didn't think they were ours. I thought, Oh, great! I'll have some gang rumble out here and be all by myself.
>
> Luckily, it was just a bunch who had gone off campus for lunch, but I didn't know that. I'll tell you, it was tense for a few minutes. Then, of course, I had to call the police back and admit the mistake. What a time.

Predicting what any new AP will experience is difficult because the shape of the assistantship varies so much from school to school. The range of structural differences alone is a surprise for APs who become administrators in schools other than where they taught. Many assume that all school management teams are structured alike:

Even though I was a teacher at another school in *this* district, I don't think we ever do two things the same way. The attendance slips, the hall passes, are all different. The AP duties are different. Every single routine in the school is different, I think, so I don't have any background, any knowledge to fall back on.

Even when counselors, deans, or teachers on special assignment pick up some responsibility for discipline, feelings of isolation are not necessarily reduced. In fact, unless there is true consistency in the way all members of the group handle discipline, the inconsistency itself is isolating.

Many APs begin their careers believing that the procedures for administering discipline are reasonably standard. Once in the office, they discover something else. Whatever it says on paper, the interplay of student characteristics, mitigating circumstances, and approaches to discipline lead to different consequences for identical infractions. Despite the confusion this difference generates in their adjustment, it takes more nerve than most beginners have to question the inconsistencies (Ashford & Cummings, 1983; C. D. Fisher, 1986; D. C. Fisher, 1986).

Newcomers are anxious to show their peers and superiors that they can learn quickly and adjust easily (Wheeler, 1966). To ask too many questions is to jeopardize an image of competence; to question too many value judgments is to invite criticism and open a gulf between the novice and the veteran. Given the contradictions that surround them, new APs frequently develop their own standards and prepare to defend them against criticism. Not only does this worsen the inconsistency in discipline administration, but it also can further intensify the new AP's isolation:

The lack of consistency surprised me. I was really apprehensive about how to discipline a kid. We have several APs, and I don't know what they all do with a student who, for example, says "fuck" to a teacher. Is "Oh, fuck!" the same infraction as "Fuck you!"? I'd spend a lot of time asking someone else every time I got a referral, and I'd get one answer from this person, another from another, another from the

principal himself. So I just said, fuck it. [laughs] I'm going to
do as I see fit and see if they'll back me.

Unlike creating a master schedule or writing a new curriculum,
discipline has no overall closure. Even graduation does not signal the
end of discipline administration. The departure of a graduating class
with its known problems also marks the entry of a new class with
unknown problems.

Discipline does not diminish over time, but usually it is punctuated
by enough successes to allow APs to feel as if they have made a
difference and that there are rewards for their investments of time and
emotion. Discipline administration is not all frustration, anger, and
disappointment. Some interventions have an impact on a student's
life, and APs recognize different kinds of growth in themselves:

I had an experience on my third day as AP that I'll never forget.
I was walking the campus, and I came on a young man
smoking behind the gym. Being the highly trained AP I am, I
asked for some identification (which he didn't have), then I
asked him to report to my office (which he didn't do). I started
a campus search and finally found him sitting in the stadium
bleachers. This time, I personally escorted him to my office.
Mission accomplished, right?

He was a junior, and I gave him my best advice on the woes
of smoking. I also informed him that he was breaking the law.
I really lit into him about ignoring me earlier, too, and that I
was suspending him more for defiance than for smoking. I'm
filling out the suspension form and, all at once, he drops his
head and starts to cry. That got to me. This big kid who had
been such a bastard up 'til then, sitting there crying. When I
asked what was going on, he began to unload his whole story.
Here's what he'd had in the previous 90 days: His father left
home; so now it was just him, his mom, and his younger
brother. They all were having a hard time, and there'd been
some ugly arguments with his mother and his brother. He was
caught shoplifting. His mother picked him up at the police
station, and then there was a very bad scene at home. But the
worst part was that he was so depressed. He'd taken all his

mother's Valium and ended up in the emergency room to have his stomach pumped.

I started having real compassion for this student, and I knew I had to do something for him immediately. Remember, now, I'm not trained for this. So I called the psychologist at the district for assistance. Instead of help, I got a 20-minute lecture about a school psych's job description: They don't do crises! They test students. They do IEPs. They do assessments, etcetera, etcetera, etcetera. Christ! They don't do anything that can really help someone.

In the meantime, I still had this young man in front of me. I called his mother at work. She was very concerned and came to my office after school, where the three of us talked for more than 3 hours. Can you believe that? We talked about everything pertaining to family, the importance of living, emotional trauma, self-esteem, present and future goals, and on and on.

Needless to say, I didn't suspend the boy. I feel like I helped him and helped his family. I learned a lot, and I felt good that I got him talking to his mother and that by the time they left, he was willing to talk to a counselor. But, I don't know if I'll ever talk to a school psych again.

At other times, the satisfactions are far less altruistic, but they are equally representative of the AP's world. They do not promote the long-range feelings of major contributions to a young person's quality of life, but they do make the moment sweet:

The call came in that somebody in the west hall boys' bathroom had blown a toilet all to hell with a cherry bomb. It was just a miracle that nobody got hurt. I mean, there was porcelain everywhere. It really dented up the stall. There was water all over, and the smoke was enough to make you choke. It happened right at the change of periods going into the last period of the day, and I decided I was going to get the outlaw who did it.

The law allows us to offer a reward to catch whoever does damage to school property. I wrote up a note just as fast as I could and had it delivered to every room, saying that there was $150 for information leading to . . . and that all sources would be kept confidential.

I had my hopes up, but I never thought we'd get the response we did. In a few minutes, we had a boy who just *had* to see the nurse right now. Then there was someone sent to his counselor, and a couple of girls who had talked their teachers into letting them go to their lockers. Thirty minutes after I sent the note, I had the name of the kid who'd done it.

It took a while to get him to confess, and it was a messy deal because his mother's active in our PTSA, but we used that to shame him. The worst part for him was when he found out that his parents were not only going to have to pay for the new fixture, they were also going to have to reimburse us for the reward money! I'll bet he'll be 20 before he works that off.

Some new APs seem to thrive on discipline administration; others see it as a terrible burden. Most have mixed feelings but usually settle into an adjustment by the latter part of their first year:

I don't know how I feel about discipline. I have really good days, and I have really bad ones. Some days and with some kids, I feel like an avenging angel, and the worst part is that I enjoy it! Other days, I feel like I'm the national director for the Tough Love movement: "I'm doing this for your own good because you need it." I read that teenagers want structure, want rules. Sometimes it's as clear as a bell that that's what a child needs. Other times, I think they're all crazy. Kids want just the opposite; they want no rules, just freedom—and I'm the one who stands in their way.

I don't know if I have a philosophy of discipline, but I think there's right and wrong and consequences to pay for being bad. I think punishment is cleansing in some way. But when it's done, I think there's an obligation to help a student keep it from happening again. But it's hard.

It is also hard to keep from becoming cynical. Dealing with obnoxious and sometimes threatening student behavior over time has a strong effect on the outlook and attitudes of some APs:

You get cynical. You can't help it. You spend your days getting lied to. Thieves, vandals, drug sellers, druggies, bullies, jerks, inconsiderate rude little so-and-so's, and you have to straighten it all out. After a while, you're not sure you can trust any kid. I find myself looking at every student I meet as a potential problem. I just can't see them the same way I did when a new student would come into my classroom when I was a teacher. That's why I think it's really important to be involved in positive things. Without that, you're going to forget what good kids are like. I can't believe I'd ever feel that way.

Even if APs do not become cynics, it is common that their outlook changes. As a result, some APs question their own sensitivity and what they think the job may be doing to them. As one woman explained:

I hardly believe anything I'm told anymore. I was at a hearing last week for a student who had a knife in the bathroom with another student. He was a special ed kid. I voted for expulsion; no question about it. Last year, as an activities person, I probably would have looked and seen that this was his first offense, saw he had pretty good grades, and Mom said he was a nice kid. But this year, what I saw was a kid who took somebody else's lunch in the bathroom, and after he had taken the lunch, showed a knife, although he had no intent to use it. When he came to the hearing, his pants were sagging halfway down his rear end, and he was dressed as a gangster. So I'm a little harder. I just hope that through the years I don't get to a point where I'm insensitive. I'm surprised I even think that way. I've always been such a kid person and kid advocate.

Sometimes a new AP sees this kind of change as adaptive behavior that helps keep things in perspective:

A really good friend in my neighborhood is a narcotics cop, and he asked me, "How do you like your new job? What's it like?" And I said, "I think it's a lot like your job. I'm eating more doughnuts and chasing bad guys." [laughs] He laughed. Seriously, I think there's a parallel. I wouldn't want to do this forever, but I can do it for now. I know I just have to arrange things so I can get to see some students who aren't bad guys.

New Perspectives and Relationships

Working With Teachers

The web of our life is of a mingled yarn, good and ill together.
Shakespeare, *All's Well That Ends Well*

L ate on a November afternoon, as we met with an assistant principal, an agitated custodian interrupted to ask her to check out a
classroom. We walked together to the room in the English wing. It
looked ravaged. Desks were covered by etched graffiti, and candy
wrappers, empty cups, half-eaten apples, and sunflower seed husks
were strewn across the floor. A sign next to the chalkboard read NO
FOOD OR DRINK ALLOWED IN THIS CLASSROOM.

"I thought I understood teachers," she said, gesturing to the mess.
"I mean, for God's sake, I've been a teacher for 13 years. But I sure
don't understand all of them. We have people who are responsible
and inspiring, selfless, and wonderful to work with. Then I go in the
next room and . . ." She paused to straighten a desk, and a Coke can
rolled out. She sighed, "It's a mystery to me why some are so much
one way and some so much another."

Most of the new APs with whom we spoke talked of the same
feeling. Their experiences varied greatly, but they carried two common themes: (a) The ranges of quality and attitude among teachers
are greater than new APs ever saw in themselves or in their teaching

colleagues; and (b) even though they are barely removed from the classroom themselves, their relationships with teachers are almost always fundamentally and permanently altered.

The Range of Teacher Behavior

Many new APs are surprised by the breadth of teacher behavior simply because they have never seen it before. The talents, skills, and attitudes that other teachers daily bestow or inflict on their students and coworkers were largely hidden from them when they were also teachers. Most secondary school teachers, especially in high schools, seldom see their colleagues perform; some never see any. Instructors who work in teaching teams regularly observe others practicing their art, but only those few. Because it is so rare for any secondary teacher to ever visit—let alone spend a sustained period of time in—other teachers' classes, very few have a clear understanding of how teaching quality and classroom climates vary throughout a building (Feiman-Nemser & Floden, 1986; McLaughlin, Talbert, & Bascia, 1990).

Sooner or later, however, job responsibilities lead APs to open every door in the school. Over time, the things they see and hear cause them to widen their definitions of what constitutes high- and low-quality performance, both within and outside the classroom. The APs who spoke with us drew from several sources in reaching their conclusions about teachers individually and collectively. The common assessment was that the quality of teaching and teachers was both better and worse than anticipated:

> I'm surprised at how much good teaching I see. The teachers in my observation pool are strong. I thought I had maybe four or five that were pretty weak, but that was from what I'd heard, not from what I'd seen. When I got into their classrooms and watched them interact with kids, they were fantastic. Out of the 12, I only had 1 that I had to put down even one negative thing on. I was really surprised at the rapport they all had with kids. Even the kind of squirrelly kids were made to feel like, "Hey, I'd better shape up for this teacher and not get out of hand."

The new APs we met during fall semesters generally reported seeing surprisingly high levels of teaching. So impressed were they that we began to wonder at how selective their experiences might have been. It is possible, of course, that a lot more good teaching goes on in secondary schools than many people assume, but it also may be that principals tend to assign to new APs the supervision and evaluation of better teachers to allow them time to become familiar with the evaluation process before facing a difficult situation.

New APs related more negative stories of teacher behavior during spring meetings than they had reported in the fall. Even before the end of their first semester, some seemed to sense that they had not been exposed to the full range of teacher behavior. In a mid-November conversation, one of them thought aloud:

> I'm very impressed by what I've seen: the amount of instruc-
> tion going on, and the time on task, the teaching methods.
> Overall, I think it's been way above what I expected. I'm a little
> skeptical going into the drop-ins [unannounced teacher obser-
> vations] because sometimes I think, I was a teacher, and I
> know when the administrators were coming, I wanted the
> lesson to be good and appropriate. And I know that's what
> I've seen so far. I'm eager to do the drop-ins and see if I'm still
> impressed.

As the term progresses, the first-year APs we talked with seemed to find their attention drawn more and more to teachers with less expertise. Their appreciation of teaching quality decreased as they came to think of teaching as more than just subject matter presentation. Some of the classroom practices new APs report seeing are enough to shake anyone's initial view of teachers. One woman told us:

> I had an experience with one of our industrial arts teachers
> teaching math. He doesn't have a full enough schedule in
> industrial arts to have a full day, so he gets stuck with a couple
> of math [classes]. He was teaching the math class at the
> beginning of the year in a regular math room. He asked if he
> could move the class to the auto shop because it was too
> difficult for him to lock it up quickly and get to the other room

and then unsecure it and start up again very fast. I said okay, but I should've thought about it more.

So a couple of days later, I walked into the math class and he had the students jammed into one small space in the shop, with all kinds of auto parts and oil and stuff all around. His disciplinary policy was that if a student was tardy, he or she was exiled to the hoist area to sit on a stool, with no books, and *under the hoist!* With a car up on it!

Judgment errors cross all department lines:

I couldn't believe he gave this survey. Our biology curriculum in the third quarter has a unit on reproduction, including human reproduction. He gave his students a survey on their sex lives. He never asked anybody before he did it—just did it. Fortunately, I heard about it from a student and went to see him before he got through the whole day with it. I was able to keep him from doing it the last two periods. You would think he was brand new to be so dumb, but he wasn't—he's been teaching here for almost 10 years. And this is the same guy who told the parents on open house night that girls almost always get better grades in his class than boys do. And he's single! The dumb shit!

New APs often find teacher supervision and evaluation more difficult than they had expected. Because they had been supervised and evaluated when they were teachers, one might think they would have a pretty good handle on what is involved. That was not the case. Teachers concentrate on their own performance as instructors while being evaluated and forget that the supervisor is also performing. The supervisor has two delicate tasks to accomplish: (a) gather data and (b) communicate evaluation results. Both take planning and attention that are not easily seen by the teacher, especially if they are well done.

Gathering the data is not just a matter of finding time to get to the teacher's classroom, although most new APs told us that was a major challenge. The process of the observation itself looks very different when viewed from the other side of the desk. New administrators frequently are surprised at the specificity and sophistication of many secondary school subjects and how difficult it is to assess the teaching of subjects about which they have absolutely no content or process knowledge. One woman, a former art teacher, summed up the feelings of several:

> Have you ever tried scripting? All teachers in our training simulations spoke at reasonable rates. I don't think real teachers talk that way. And if a discussion really gets going in a class, the exchanges are just too quick to record. Other times, I'm also trying to see how the teacher is spreading contact around the room, if they're getting everyone engaged. If they're good at it, my eyes are flying all over the room. And, in some classes, it's like trying to keep up in a foreign language. I mean, it *is* a foreign language in our French and Latin classes. But it is just about as foreign in calculus and physics. So are advanced computer classes and the upper levels of industrial and automotive technology. I just don't have the vocabulary. I don't know whether the content is accurate or even the most appropriate. I have to guess at whether a student gets the answer to the question by watching their behavior. I don't know if the answer is right or wrong in terms of content, let alone whether it's the best answer or whether there's a better way to explain or demonstrate it. It takes a lot of attitude and behavior interpretation on my part.

The difficulties can be compounded by the evaluation system the district has negotiated. Depending on the specific model, new APs observing teachers may be involved in a multiplicity of activities in their attempts to see, record, and assess teacher classroom performance. Some appraisal systems require observers to look for a variety of lesson components and teacher-student and student-student interactions. New APs are sometimes almost overwhelmed by how many things there are to look for simultaneously in teacher observation. "It's hard," one man told us:

> I feel like I used to feel when I was teaching driver training out in the car. I'm trying to see where we're going, how we're

standing in relation to others on the road, how much the driver knows, how steady he is, how well he can see what's coming up ahead, how well he makes turns, how well he knows what's going on around him, when to slow down, when to speed up, when to stop, how to stop. I guess it's really more like it would be to try to teach someone school bus driver training. I have to do all those things and watch 30 passengers at the same time to see if they're understanding where we're going and enjoying the ride.

One aspect of teacher supervision and evaluation that new APs seem least prepared for is the human element. People are always sensitive to evaluation. Despite having been teachers, having had university training, and usually having some district-level in-service work on teacher evaluation, the differences between simulations and actual evaluations are stark, and the emotions they evoke are strong. One woman's feelings about teacher evaluation were representative:

I knew it was part of my job. I expected to dislike it, and I *hate* it! But I'll do it. I enjoy visiting classrooms, and I enjoy interacting with teachers, and I enjoy the good evaluations, I guess, but I hate the hard ones. I know it's my responsibility to evaluate accurately what I see, and that's not always easy. And it's my responsibility to share it with a teacher, and I think my greatest dislike for it—maybe it's a fear—is how they're going to receive it and how they're going to accept my suggestions. So I guess the reason I hate it is because it's tense for me.

Most new APs remember their own feelings when they were observed and are aware that the very thought of observation and evaluation makes some teachers nervous. Still, perhaps because they were strong teachers themselves, some new APs are surprised by the nervousness even some experienced teachers exhibit:

One of the things I was surprised by was how nervous some teachers were when I told them we needed to set up a conference because I had to evaluate them, 'cause I don't see myself as an intimidating person; I see myself as a person to support them. And I guess when you say, "You're going to be evaluated," it just brings on a certain amount of anxiety, and I was kind of shocked that *I* was causing that anxiety. I really don't see myself as that kind of person. I don't go out to "get" anybody.

In some cases, the surprise is connected with the fact that the new APs have not yet had time to fully develop an image of themselves as administrators. Perhaps teachers perceive the change in status and the authority that comes with it before some new administrators have fully taken on the role. This possibility is suggested by the comments of one man who became an AP in the same school where he taught:

> Some of their reactions were a surprise. There are some teachers I thought I could be very open and honest with. I could tell them how I felt because I was relating to them teacher to teacher. I've known them for years. I really thought they were seeing me as one of them, but they weren't. They were seeing me as the administrator, and I didn't feel like an administrator.

Communicating descriptions and assessments of teacher performance is a delicate art. Words have to be chosen carefully. The evaluator's challenge is to clarify the situation and to communicate the perceived gap between what a person is doing and what ought to happen so that the person being evaluated will accept the assessment and want to change (Jablin, 1984). It is a skill that many new APs take a long time to develop:

> I never realized how difficult it is to put into words what you're seeing and what's wrong and what needs to be improved. It's not at all like telling a student what needs to be done. Things I did as a teacher, I did intuitively. So I'm finding it very difficult, much more difficult than I had imagined, to take those things, which to me are very obvious, and put words to them. But I have to do that when I confer with teachers—give direction and suggestions for improvement. God, it's hard, and I think it may be a long time before I become effective at it.

Evaluation goals have to be considered within the context of a continuing relationship. Feedback is best given and received in an atmosphere of trust (Duke & Stiggins, 1988). A trusting atmosphere takes time to build, and it simply does not exist for brand new administrators and the teachers they evaluate. Over time, trust can grow, but the first-year AP has to operate without it, which many find difficult:

> Evaluation in this district is tied to clinical supervision. And it's sort of an oil-and-water mixture. Clinical supervision is a teacher improvement system, but evaluation carries that heavy thud of "you could be fired." They don't go together. You want to go in there and win the confidence of the teachers so they'll have the courage to try new things, but they also say to themselves, "If I don't succeed in these things, that's going to be written up in my formal evaluation. So, I'll stick with what's tried and true, because that's what's worked for me."

Another difficulty some new APs have with teacher evaluation is a doubt that it is worth the intellectual and emotional investment required of both teacher and administrator. Research suggests that many teachers, especially the more experienced, have no confidence that supervision and evaluation will help them improve (Center for Public Interest Polling, 1986; Koppich, Gerritz, & Guthrie, 1986). As administrators, many new APs wonder whether evaluation really will make any difference in the long run:

> A few observations, and it's over with. Can that be valuable to a teacher? I don't know. Even though I spend a lot of time and energy on the evaluation process, I don't know how valuable it is. For me as a teacher, it was just there. It was supposed to be really important, but . . . And I look at it now, and I think, I don't know what kind of impact it has on the teacher.
>
> The things that really count in teaching can't be measured in our system. One teacher asked me, "What can you really tell from one period?" I gave him the answers we were trained to give, but I feel like such a hypocrite.

Whether these new APs are right or wrong about teacher evaluation is immaterial. Their feelings are their own, and these sentiments surfaced often enough to suggest that doubts about the evaluation process and about their own competencies are a common part of the first-year experience.

The reservations that new APs hold about the evaluation process often are reinforced when good teachers, especially tenured master teachers, share the same doubts:

> What do I tell a teacher like [name]? She knows she's good. I know she's good. She plays the game with me: has the preconference, lets me come and watch her teach, and sits through the postobservation conference. It's a waste of all our time. At least [she] is nice about it. The problem is, it's just about as much of a waste of time with most of our average teachers. They're anxious when I come to the classroom, but most of them are pretty cool in the conference afterward. Unless the lesson was simply a disaster, they know I don't really have any leverage to make them change very much.

Some teachers take no responsibility for the things APs have to look for in evaluations:

> I had one teacher tell me that of course his evaluation was bad. He has the worst kids in the school. He used to get good evaluations, but he isn't getting the kind of students he used to get. Part of it is that the principal doesn't like him and he isn't getting the higher level students he used to get, but part of it is that kids have just changed. They don't want to learn, and they don't want to work, and they won't behave. Students used to be better behaved, and he used to have better support from the administration. He completely rejected my argument that he had to change his approach with changing conditions.

Sometimes, fortunately not too frequently, teacher defense mechanisms lead to behavior that is truly surprising, clearly contemptuous

of the process, and destructive of any long-range, positive professional relationship, as these examples of escalating severity illustrate:

> He changed what he was doing midstream, I'm sure. I came
> into his government class about 10 minutes after it began.
> When I sat down, he was going full steam with a lecture on
> the electoral college, but he didn't finish it. After only a few
> minutes, he told the students to look up three points he had
> explained to them in their textbooks and find examples. So,
> what was I supposed to do? Sit there and watch the students
> go through their books? It made me mad, but I couldn't prove
> that he did it just because I was there. But I'm sure he did. With
> all the speculation about the presidential election this year, I
> know enough about the electoral college system to know that
> where he stopped wasn't a logical place to stop.

Sometimes teachers enlist their own students as co-conspirators in
sabotaging evaluations:

> I was out on the campus today just before lunch began, and I
> saw a teacher whose class I had visited 2 days before walking
> with a large group of students, and I recognized some of the
> young people with her. I asked her where she was going, and
> she said, "I'm taking the class to lunch at a Mexican restaurant
> as a pay-off for how good they were when you came in the
> room." [laughs] And the bad thing was they weren't really that
> good. I would have thought they'd have had little halos over
> their heads in order to get that kind of reward. I thought she was
> joking when she first said it, but I don't think she was. It's sad, I
> think, but it also makes me more angry than I can tell you.

And sometimes the relationship can be poisoned forever:

> I went in October to observe [a geography teacher]. When I
> came into the room, he went outside. I went outside after him
> and asked him what he was doing. I told him I had come for
> an observation. He said he knew that, but the law required
> only one certificated person to oversee a group of students and

that if I was going to be in the room, he didn't need to be. I didn't know what to do. It had never occurred to me that someone might refuse to be observed or evaluated. I felt like a kid tattling, but I didn't think I had any choice but to go straight to the principal. There was an ugly scene between the principal and [the teacher], but it was also pretty clear to me that the principal thought I should have taken the teacher on right then.

New APs are often as surprised by how teachers vary in class-room management and discipline skills as they are by how much they vary in instructional quality. Many new APs are amazed by the number of teachers who look to the office to solve even the smallest classroom behavior problems. The surprise may stem from the new AP's own experiences as a teacher. None of those we talked with ever admitted that they had experienced classroom control difficulties. Judging by the way they perceived their own handling of student behavior problems, they often are surprised that others do not handle them as effectively as they remember themselves doing. One woman put it into perspective:

I'm surprised by the nature of the referrals, the picky little things. Who cares if they chew gum? You know, you have to wonder. You get referrals for chewing gum, and you've spent the morning with a policeman and a girl who was attacked by her stepfather. In the overall picture, who cares about the gum? I never sent anybody to the office for chewing gum. I realize the teacher wants me to be supportive of the fact that this kid was really rude, but I just wonder if it really matters that much, you know. You're trying to be supportive, and I'm telling the kid: If she asks you to dump the gum, dump the gum.

Another new AP echoed the feeling:

I guess I always thought that teachers were all pretty confident, assertive types of individuals. And when I went into activities, I started to realize that there were a lot of teachers who didn't feel as comfortable as I. There're a lot of teachers who have a fear of contacting a home, and that surprised me. Now it really is a surprise as an AP. I do it all the time. Teachers just don't want to deal with parents. That's a surprise. Most teachers are parents. This is a professional response, but even as a parent, wouldn't you expect the same courtesy?

Teacher behavior in a school, of course, is not limited to the classroom or to interactions with students. Many new APs are surprised at the level of conflict they find between teachers as individuals and as groups. Perhaps one of the talents or characteristics that leads to an AP appointment is an ability to work with and get along with others. This ability could explain why so many of the new APs with whom we worked were surprised that they had never been aware of the myriad deep currents of conflict that often characterize secondary school settings.

It is difficult to escape the conclusion that secondary school departmentalization contributes to interunit and interpersonal conflict. Research has shown that secondary teachers identify professionally with their subject matter department more than with the school as an entity (Johnson, 1990). The very fact that secondary schools deal in subject matter disciplines ensures that the intellectual interests and classroom experiences of teachers across departments vary anywhere from slightly to significantly. These differences cause departments to function as subcultures in the school (Siskin, 1991). While holding in common the values of the larger school culture, discipline-based subcultures incorporate additional values and generate norms that are not shared by colleagues in other departments or divisions.

Identification with a subgroup rather than with the school organization as a whole heightens the potential for conflict, and the experience of new APs suggests that the potential often is fulfilled. The competition for recognition and resources in secondary schools can be fierce. The new APs with whom we spoke described interdepartmental conflicts that fit Pondy's (1967) classic typology of conflict resulting from (a) competition for scarce resources, including clientele; (b) the attempts of one department to control the activities "belonging" to another, such as conflict between the Math and Science Departments over how and how much math to incorporate into science classes; and (c) conflict resulting from two parties in the organization, such as counseling and an academic department, that must work together but cannot agree on how to do so because of competing goals. One high school AP told us:

> We have a real problem between the Counseling Department and the Social Studies Department. When students are kicked out of a social studies class for low grades or poor attendance or, worse, for discipline reasons, the counselors try to immediately place them in another social studies class so they won't fall behind in their requirements. The social studies teachers say that they shouldn't have to bear the burden for a student's inability to get along with another teacher or help him escape the consequences of his action. If a student is thrown out of one social studies class, the other teachers of the same subject refuse to accept him into one of their classes. It puts me in a bad spot, though they more often appeal it to the principal. Either way I decide, I make someone mad at me.

Some of the conflicts are even completely divorced from academics and focus on concerns only tangential to the classroom:

> The Performing Arts Department is always wanting something from someone: kids released for band or orchestra practice or play practice, or people to buy tickets to something or another. But the teachers in that department just about refuse to help any of the other departments with any of their fundraisers. They don't even help much with the PTSA membership drive or the holiday food project. You can't believe the ill feeling that causes and how it spills over into all kinds of other activities and meetings. It's worse, sometimes, than dealing with the kids.

Much of the conflict between teachers probably can be attributed to goal divergence (Pondy, 1967), but some of it is simply personality. As one new AP described it:

> It was a real eye-opener that some teachers can be so uncooperative and rude, and not just to me, but to each other. I was

surprised by the staff conflict. I work with one man here who has a perfect record: He's never missed an opportunity either to offend or to be offended.

The Development of
New Working Relationships

People are defined by the jobs they hold. Those who accept administrative authority and responsibility are no longer perceived as fellow teachers, regardless of the new administrator's continuing commitment to the students, curriculum, and instruction—the stuff of the classroom. A change in status by definition means a change in the working relationship. As obvious as this seems, many new APs still are surprised when teachers no longer treat them as one of their own.

Research demonstrates that it takes time for people to become socialized to a managerial job and to redefine themselves in its terms (Louis, 1980; Nicholson & West, 1988), but it probably does not take much time for those who remain in the ranks to redefine the person who moves into the office. Having a preexisting notion of what APs are like and how they should behave, staff members may begin immediately to apply their standards and expectations to the new administrator. When this takes place, beginning administrators often are surprised by how they are treated. The intensity of the surprise may have its roots in the perceptions held by administrators when they were still teachers. Many of the APs with whom we spoke indicated they had always been on good terms with administrators. Possibly, teachers who aspire to administration perceive less of a difference between themselves and administrators than those who do not, certainly less than those who see administrators as adversaries or impediments.

If true, these ideas help explain the immediate change in relationships between teachers and new administrators, changes initiated the moment a new AP's appointment is announced. A frequent theme in our conversations with new assistants was how quickly and deeply they sensed a distance from their former colleagues. Those who became administrators where they had taught were particularly sensitive to their new outsider status:

I was surprised that I was treated differently even before I actually went into the office. The minute you are selected, the change begins, not when you take the job. All at once there was a little veil between us. This was a shock to me. People who had been pretty close didn't talk to me as freely as they had before. Then a friend said to me, "You're different; you're an administrator."

A sense of loss was apparent in one woman's remarks:

I had a friend come over here who has been a counselor at another school. She and I have been friends for years, and she was sitting in the teachers' lounge in the smoking section, waiting for me to arrive. I don't smoke, so when I opened the door and went in, I pretended like I was coughing and hacking. She looked up at me and said, "Aaah, shut up!" I glanced at the teachers out of the corner of my eye and, well, their mouths dropped open. But this is what I miss! I was always one of the guys before, and people never had a second thought about teasing me.

Another AP told us how he missed being part of the teacher group:

There was a group of us, and one of us used to go to a local bakery every Friday morning to buy big gooey Napoleons and cream puffs and things like that to eat at the break. We never talked much about teaching, but we did talk a lot about what was going on in the school and district and how we felt about it. Now when I go into the coffee room at the break, I can almost hear them say, "Quiet! Here he comes" when I approach.

As if adjusting to social distancing from most teachers were not enough, new APs must adjust to the flattery and overstated displays of respect and affection of those who try to build influence. One man indicated his disgust:

It's the phonies who bug me! Those people who think they have to talk to me now, be friendly. One person who hadn't used my first name in years came in today and did it. It turned out he wanted to go to a conference and wanted my signature. It's all based on their idea that being nice is going to get them something. I wasn't surprised with him so much, but I was by how many others do it too.

An AP responsible for guidance services and the master schedule voiced a suspicion:

The surprise is *who* would be trying to exert influence on me now that I'm supposed to be somebody with a lot of power. They're saying, "Oh, you're one of the administrators now. You can solve this." But they're thinking, "What do I want from him, and how can I get it?"

An AP who changed schools to become an administrator observed:

Either the teachers in this school are a lot nicer than the people where I worked before, or this is a honeymoon period, or they see a chance to score points with the new kid on the block, but there are an awful lot of very friendly people here who all want to tell me things in confidence, show me how things are done, and help me in any way they can. I'm not usually very cynical, I don't think, but I remember one of my mentors telling me never to trust an old enemy or a new friend. That may be good advice.

These are relatively common behaviors in managerial turnover situations. The arrival of a new AP poses the possibility of a substantial change in the way a particular office operates and how the incumbent relates to staff members. The greater the ambiguity in a situation, the higher the probability that people will take advantage of opportunities to promote or protect their self-interests or use influence-building tactics (Ferris & Kacmar, 1988; Ralston, 1985).

Whether they were dealing with teachers who showed them distant respect or teachers who tried to buy their way into a relationship, new APs did not know when they first took office how much resistance there could be to their authority or how much informal influence they might have. Many were pleasantly surprised to discover the ease with which they could exercise their authority when they tried. Accustomed to the casual level of attention their remarks received as teachers, some were impressed by how others listened to them simply because of their positions. A guidance, attendance, and discipline AP explained:

> I think I was surprised by the authority they give the position in a way. I mean, sometimes I'll say something offhand, and it's taken so seriously; it seems to have such import to the people it was said to. So now I've learned to watch what I'm saying.

Another woman, midway through her first year, expressed a tangential experience:

> I'm surprised at the influence. People, even though they don't know me beyond the 5 or 6 months I've been in this job, come to me and look to me for leadership. And I'm sure I got, initially, the status or buy-in from the faculty because of the position, but I also think it's because I follow through on things. But I think the position title buys you a lot of time to either screw up or do a good job. [laughs]

New APs must recognize not only that what they say will have more impact on other adults than previously but also that they now are expected to assert their new authority. One AP described the experience this way:

> When I took the job, I didn't perceive myself any differently, and yet other people perceived me as an administrator. Well, I had a hard time dealing with that. I wasn't sure, now that I was working with adults primarily and not students, and I was real hesitant. So, I sat back an awful lot, just sort of expecting other people to take the initiative. And I'd be invited to meetings and everyone, you know, would be sitting at the desk and sort of turn around and say, "Okay, run the meeting." It was with things like that that I just began to react, and then

I kind of made it over a hump in terms of relating to people. I'm beginning now to perceive myself as an administrator with the responsibilities that go along with the job.

New APs commonly remark they are surprised to discover that they work in an environment where they think others expect them to know all of the answers and to be able to do whatever needs to be done. One woman described it this way:

They expect me to be able to do anything and to do it just because I can or because they think I can. It's *my* responsibility to solve *their* problems. I always took care of my own problems when I was a teacher. I didn't go running to the administration every time something went wrong. God, I get tired of that. I don't know if it's just the people in this school or if it's like that everywhere.

One of her male counterparts reported similar feelings, which indicated that it may be "like that everywhere," when he said, "All of a sudden, you're supposed to know everything. I would tell people, 'Look, I'm just finishing my first week. I have a lot to learn.' "

Staff members also surprise new APs with their reduced tolerance when APs make mistakes or show insensitivities:

I'm amazed at how different the standards are. I have teachers who screw up purchase orders, don't get grades in on time, don't show up where they're supposed to, or really mishandle a kid. They expect it to be handled privately and to be forgiven and the incident put behind them. I make a mistake, and I get a flood of complaints, and they complain about it to the principal. It gets talked about all over the building, and every-body seems to remember it.

I guess I know it's just because administrative mistakes are more visible, and a screwup with a schedule or buses or facilities affects a lot of people all at once, but somehow it just doesn't seem fair. And, of course, some people sit out there like vultures, waiting for you to make a mistake, and then enjoying it when you do. I don't think I'll ever get used to that.

Another AP thought the situation reached its peak for her when a teacher actually yelled at her:

> This is a new thing for me: "Excuse me. You're yelling at me?" I hadn't been yelled at in the classroom. I was not the kind of person kids yelled at. I mean, they yell at you for things you don't have control of, as well as for things you do. Yesterday, the teachers were mad at the principal because he had changed the calendar and scheduled a meeting at 2:00 on a grading day [during finals week], and all at once there's someone yelling at me. And I said, "You know, I found out when you found out. I got the notice in my mailbox. The principal was gone to a PTA breakfast." And he'd left me here to catch the flak.

Some try to take it philosophically, but it is difficult. One man responsible for guidance thought he understood why many teachers have the attitudes they do, but he still didn't like it:

> Sometimes it's the backlash of low morale over time, the sins of others that you have to endure. I think it's a real surprise how much the feeling about the office survives the individuals who pass through it. You're the only one they can vocalize to, and you understand that. It's the office they're reacting to, not you. On my *third day here*, a woman I worked with as a department chair when I was in science, in *my own* department, asked me, "Has it really been that long that you've been out of the classroom?" You know what I told her? "Cheap shot!"

The experience of becoming an AP clearly illustrates what research tells us about personal and professional transitions. Relationships with former colleagues are inevitably redefined. This happens partly because new administrators are exposed to new information, develop new and broader perspectives about both the organization and the specific work they used to do, and experience a change in status that invests them with greater authority and responsibility. It also happens partly because their former colleagues will have it no other way.

New Perspectives and Relationships
Working With the Classified Staff

I was a stranger and ye took me in.
Matthew 25:35

"I would be dead without my secretary." The assistant principal
indicated a plump, middle-aged woman who sat behind her
desk in the main hallway, phone receiver cradled against her
shoulder as she worked on inputting data to a computer screen. "I
thought I knew how things worked, but there were an awful lot of
things I didn't know anything about." The secretary no sooner
hung up the phone than it rang again. This time, she held it to the
opposite ear, hardly missing a beat on the computer. The AP shook
his head admiringly. "She's a one-woman triage system."

As much as new APs are surprised by what they discover about
teachers, at least they come into the job understanding faculty roles.
They have a sense of what faculty members do, how it ought to be
done, and they know the limits and opportunities of the classroom.
New administrators, of course, must redefine their relationships with
those who were previously their peers, but the key word is redefine.
In their first dealings with classified staff members, most new APs
must create relationships; they have no experience on which to draw.

Classroom teachers do not have secretaries. Some schools provide clerical assistants, but the clerk who types exams or makes copies serves an entire corps of teachers. Even the comparatively few new APs who were counselors, coordinators, or activity directors and had clerical support usually enjoyed only a share of the secretary's time. It is a new experience to have a secretary who attends to their particular needs and gives priority to their work. Neither do they have experience in establishing relationships with other clerical staff members. Teachers only sporadically interact with clerical personnel and are rarely responsible for their supervision or evaluation.

Relationships between teachers and operations or custodial staff members are also usually infrequent. Depending on the size of the school, teachers may know custodians by sight or by name, but few have consistent, let alone daily, interaction with them—even less than with the clerical staff. Maintenance and operation crew members on the day shift, except on rare occasions, perform their duties away from the classrooms. The afternoon- and evening-shift custodians who clean the building do their work after the teachers leave.

The relationship between teachers and food service workers is even more distant. Secretaries, clerks, aides, and custodians all have some attachment, albeit tenuous, to what goes on in the classroom, but food service workers do not. Rarely are kitchen staff members recognized as participants in the educational enterprise. Although teachers may recognize the cooks and servers who labor in the school cafeteria, they usually have no contact with them outside meal hours. Pouring a cup of coffee in the morning or dishing up a lunch plate takes only a moment; teachers get their food and move on.

New APs often are surprised to find that classified staff members play such important roles in secondary schools. For most of the new APs with whom we spoke, discovery of the volume, variety, stressfulness, and importance of the work done by the classified staff was both surprising and enlightening. Perhaps more important, new APs are often equally surprised by the kind of power certain classified staff members can wield and how much new APs depend on them in the socialization process.

Discovering the
Support Staff's Work World

An AP for student activities, who had a good view of the classified staff by working daily with both clerical and operations crews, put it this way:

> I knew I couldn't run this office without those people, but I didn't know how much they do and all the time. We couldn't run an athletic program without the help of my secretary and the clerks in here. I never realized how much work went into just one game, and I'm not even talking about insurance papers, student physicals, parent permissions, all the correspondence with other schools in the league and the league office, and all the other things that must happen in advance, and not just once. They happen over and over with every sport in every season. And that doesn't scratch the surface. Then there's all the work done to set up for a game or a meet. The operations crew is vital to me: fields prepared, mats down, nets up, bleachers cleaned and opened, locker rooms, showers, concessions set up, it goes on and on. It's phenomenal. And I used to just walk into the gym and think a basketball game was fun. Then they clean it all up so the facility can be used by PE classes or some community group the next morning. I'd really be up a creek if they didn't do their jobs as well as they do.

Another AP, responsible for student attendance and welfare, saw equally crucial service rendered every day in her office:

> I used to just take roll and send the roll sheet down to the office. I had no idea of what happened then. Every hour, they're handling the roll sheets from a hundred rooms, literally. And while they're trying to process those, they're interrupted every other minute by some phone call from a parent or a teacher or someone else to report an absence or to ask about policy or to clear up an unexcused absence or to complain or for something else. Then there are students and

parents and teachers who come into the office to find out
something or to get something. Every student who's absent
has to come to the attendance office and get a re-admit slip
before he or she can go back to class. You'd think all that would
be taken care of first thing in the morning, but there are kids
coming into and going out of this school all day. One needs a
re-admit, and a minute later there's another one who needs an
off-grounds permit.

Then they're always giving me lists of truants who need to
be confronted, or names of students with excessive absences
of one kind or another, and students who are being admitted
to school or withdrawing from school. Then they're compiling
weekly reports about attendance, and monthly accounting to
the district office, and other reports to the county or state. It's
mind-boggling what they do. And they catch hell from rude kids
and irate parents before they ever get to me. And they supervise
student helpers, and that's often a problem. We had a student
steal blank re-admit forms so she and her friends could write
their own excuses and get back into class without anyone
knowing they were gone. They had to deal with that. Give me
a minute, and I'll think of more things they do. See, those are
everyday things. They also help with registration in the fall
and graduation in the spring. It's just amazing what they do.

Change the name of the office from attendance to guidance, and
new APs who supervise counseling services give an equally long list
of reasons why their clerical staff is so important to office operations.
Change the name of the office again to plant management or curriculum or staff development or discipline or to any other unit, and new
APs are similarly surprised at the volume and importance of the
work done by the classified staff.

The pressures on classified staff members are frequently high.
Not only are they often the first employees to encounter the public, but
some of their work is more visible to parents and community members
than it is to many school employees. Late or inaccurate mailings,
error-ridden schedules, buses that do not arrive on time, deficiencies in
facility setup or cleanup, and other mistakes draw immediate reactions from parents and community groups. Staff members are often

accountable to multiple supervisors, and they are pressured to give priority to each one's work. Usually less-educated and noncertificated, they represent a subordinate class in the school and sometimes are denied the level of respect professional staff members receive from students, parents, and the faculty. The consensus among the new APs with whom we spoke was that there is a hierarchy of classified staff members, with janitors at the bottom and confidential secretaries at the top. One AP responsible for evaluating the support staff explained how he discovered it:

> I thought I would have monthly meetings with the classified staff just like the principal has monthly faculty meetings. I thought it would open communication lines and make these employees feel more a part of the school. I required the clerical and operations staff to attend and invited all the others. I was really surprised by the outcome. First, only those required to come came. Second, about 95% of the questions and statements came from the clerical staff. The custodians and grounds people just wouldn't say much at all. No operations person ever disagreed with anything any of the clerks or secretaries said, and it was real clear to me that the clerks were deferring to the secretaries. After 2 months, I started holding separate meetings for clerical and custodial staffs. The difference is something to see.

The hierarchy also is reflected in the way the district personnel treat the classified staff. Maintenance and operations are usually the first to have their ranks reduced in times of budgetary shortfalls, followed by clerks, and last by secretaries. Teachers seem aware of the hierarchy and understand that at some levels the classified force frequently is understaffed, but they often do not recognize the implications until they take on an administrative position. Although the staff may be cut, the organization and its clients still expect the same services. Many new APs are surprised by how much the classified staff is asked to do, especially in the light of cutbacks:

> We've had declining enrollment in this district, and you know that means less money. And what's the first thing that gets cut?

Maintenance and operations. But the school's still the same size, and even though we have fewer kids, we're still under pressure to keep the same athletic and activities schedules. It's hard. We've got some real sour asses, but most of them have been around here long enough that they care. They care about the place; they like it. And they do the work.

As in any group, of course, some staff members work harder than others, and some are more able. Some dazzle new APs with their commitment and competence, as one man told us:

The classified staff saved my behind just last month. We were all scheduled to have our prom at [nearby military base] officers' club. One of our teachers is a reserve officer holding a high rank. He arranged it for us, but between the time the agreement was made last fall and the time for the prom, the military changed its policy and canceled the use of the club for all outside organizations. The problem was, no one bothered to notify us—probably since we were in on an informal agreement. When the band we hired went to the club to see how they could set up on Saturday, they were told that our school didn't have any dance scheduled there; in fact, they didn't rent to any schools at all.

We got the call from the band leader at about 3:30, after all the kids had left on Friday afternoon. We had almost 350 couples planning to show up at the officers' club the next night and no way to tell them the deal was off. Of course, the deal wasn't really off. You can't just cancel a prom after dresses have been bought and tuxes rented and all the upsets about who is going to go with whom. So a second problem was to get an alternate site for the dance.

You can't get a hotel ballroom by calling up the night before you need it, so our only chance of making this work was to hold it in our gym. That meant we had to bump the community recreation group who'd rented it for Saturday night. I called the central office and told them our problem. The secretaries there were wonderful. They took care of giving the bad news to recreation and refunding their rental deposit and making amends. I got the principal to send a letter of apology later, but the district office people were the ones who caught the flak.

Then we had to contact all the kids and tell them the dance was going to be in our gym. That wasn't going to be good news. The prom is a big deal here, and what makes it a big deal is that it isn't in the gym like all the other dances. Fortunately, we had a list of everyone who'd bought a bid to the dance 'cause our activity director makes them give the name and phone number of who they're bringing, as well as their own. I had to press every secretary and clerk into service calling these kids and telling them about the change. I had ugly exchanges with a couple who said it wasn't their job, but the rest were great. We couldn't get all those calls made before their shift ended at 4:00, and most of them stayed until well after 5:00, some until 6:00, to help me track down these kids and get the word out. I don't know how we did it, but we really did do the job.

Then we still had to get the gym set up, and our custodial crew came through like champs. I talked to the head custodian. He had gone home, but he came back, and we tried to figure out what to do. It was fantastic. He said he would have a crew there Saturday morning and we'd make it work somehow. Saturday morning, I met him at the gym. He only had three of the guys, but they worked like Trojans. The spring play had been *The Music Man*, so we raided the Drama Department and stole all the props. We decided we could make the gym into a park. We took the gazebo and put it in the center of the floor for a bandstand. A couple of teachers came by to help us, then we got some kids up there to help decorate. The custodians took chain saws and cut limbs off trees and lashed them to the volleyball standards to make our own trees in the gym. I don't even want to know where all the potted plants and bushes came from. Then they found strings of Christmas lights somewhere. The long and short of it is, that if you turned the lights way down low, the gym looked like a park on a spring night. It wasn't fancy like a hotel or the officers' club, but it was okay. We got only a few complaints from some of the snooty parents, and it worked for the kids.

It never could have been done without those guys and the women in the office. You never saw anybody move more quickly on something and laugh about it. It was great! Of course, I'll never live it down. We're planning graduation now, and they keep asking if we should reserve the gym.

Part of the challenge for new APs in dealing with classified staff members is, of course, that not all of them operate at a level of excellence. One of the things that surprises many new APs is the range of ability levels, attitudes, and work ethics among the staff members. They are surprised to find more variation in teachers than they expected, but substantially more variation is found across and within classified positions. The wide spectrum of capability forces new APs to develop differentiated styles of leadership:

> I am really surprised by the wide span of adults I must deal with in the classified group. There's all different levels of intellect and ability. I must use situational leadership—take them where I find them. My secretary is brilliant. She used to be a second-grade teacher. Then I have a custodian who is functionally illiterate.

Another AP described the challenge he faces when he must deal with either a conflict between a teacher and a classified worker or when he must get them to work together on a project. One man, frustrated by some of the problems of plant management, drew a picture that others agreed with in concept, if not in emotion:

> I didn't know classified that well. You know, as a teacher you see them in passing and say hi to a janitor or secretary. But I found classified people different. I deal with the janitors 'cause I'm in charge of maintenance and operations; I deal with the grounds people, et cetera. I find them to be, in my opinion, very irresponsible. Their attendance is horrible. And they don't see it that way. Someone made a statement to me a few

years ago like "That's why they're janitors," and I thought what's with this guy? Why is he making that statement? But you know what? That would be my statement right now. That's why they're custodial help. That's why they're at a job that doesn't pay much. You have your exceptions, but over all, my opinion is that they're not very responsible people.

Now, when I talk about the clerical, they are more responsible. I must break that up into categories, so I've had some surprises in what I've thought of different categories of classified people. I like them all, and I get along with them all fairly well. But I've had to discipline some of them, and I never thought I'd be disciplining classified people. Very similar to disciplining some of the kids. Some of the mentality and actions are no more mature than some of the kids.

This AP's extreme remarks may have been a result of conditions existing only in his school, but new APs commonly are surprised by how many people regularly miss work or come late. And they frequently are surprised at how quickly union support is invoked when a classified staff member is confronted concerning inadequate performance. New APs seem to understand the tension between issues of teacher professionalism and unionism and are aware from their own experience of the role played by the negotiated contract. But many are surprised to find how contract driven are the relationships and behaviors of classified staff members. An AP for curriculum and instruction explained:

I spend a lot of time reading the contract, a lot more than I ever spent reading the teachers' contract. I have the contract on file, and all the procedures you must follow exactly. I have how you write them up, what procedures you must go through, the format for the oral reprimand. So I really study that going in. As a classroom teacher, I knew the classified had a contract, but it surprised me that it was so strong and carried out through all groups.

A frequent frustration for many new APs is that the union emphasis results in limits on what an employee can be gotten to do. An AP responsible for discipline in a school with a large Hispanic population reported that she had two clerks in her office who spoke Spanish but refused to do so in dealing with students or with the public. They had concluded that the language was a skill for which they should receive extra compensation, and because foreign language proficiency was not rewarded in that district, they refused to use it, despite the fact that parents called with all manner of questions. Most of the new APs with whom we spoke reported similar problems: groundsmen who would not help with furniture; clerks in one office not willing to help in another; strict adherence to job classification.

New APs often are surprised at the prevalence of the not-my-job attitude in their departments or schools. They usually understand contractual constraints, but the experience is still alien for them, particularly when their own responsibilities encompass so many things not mentioned in the AP job description:

> I must get our two attendance ladies and the registrar—who's in another office—to help me prepare this attendance report; there's no way I can do it by myself. The principal tells me what he needs, and I tell them what he needs, and we go over it, but it doesn't get done. And I've never had a problem before with people not doing what I tell them to do. It's driving me crazy. They think I'm a tyrant, but if I'm not dictatorial, it doesn't get finished. I must divide each portion of the task into something that clearly fits the job description of each. And I can't be watching over them every minute. I've had to take over the bus supervision and more of the discipline because the other AP has been in the hospital. I just need them to do it.

Many of the APs with whom we talked interpret this attitude as pettiness. An AP responsible for guidance, attendance, and discipline and who saw all three functions as interrelated and took a strong team approach to her work expressed how many felt:

> Some of my valuable time gets drained away with this nonsense of "Well, you know, if I place this here, I expect her to take this and file it back there, and I shouldn't have to walk

all the way to the back." And, "It's not my job. It's not in my description." That gets *very* irritating to me. Who cares if it's part of your job description or not? I mean, this is a team, and we have a job to get done, and let's get it done.

Little research has been done on the interactions of administrators and classified employees, especially in secondary schools, but there appears to be some support for what the APs reported. Young (1982), for example, identified a relationship between the interest administrators took in custodians and their level of job satisfaction. In a study involving 31 high school principals but no APs, Butler (1983) found that trust between administrator and secretary was reciprocal. To be trusted, one has to trust.

It seems a clear lesson for most first-year APs that dealing with classified staff members is, in at least one way, the same as dealing with teachers: What can be gotten as a result of exercising position power is severely limited. New APs quickly learn that, most of the time, influence bought with reciprocal respect, visible support, facilitation of effort, recognition, and a favor here and there is a much more effective tool in gaining classified staff compliance than invoking formal authority. The AP whose prom was saved by the classified staff did not get that kind of support by just enforcing the contract. Rather, he and many others told us stories of cooperation gained as a by-product of acts such as the example in simple courtesy one woman gave us:

> I was surprised at how something as small as sending a note could have an effect on some people who were known for being negative to the person who has this job, how that kind of changed their whole perspective of this office and of me.

A man gave us another example based in continued interaction:

> I'm always on supervision duty at lunchtime, so I must eat after everyone else has gone back to class. If we have a discipline incident to deal with, I get to the cafeteria late, and the place is closed up. I was losing enough weight in this job. I wanted lunch. I don't really know what happened, but one

day there was a problem in the student food line. I took care of it quickly, and then I took cafeteria duty myself for the next week, and I got to talking and laughing with the ladies in there. The next week, I came in after lunch one day, starving. I went into the kitchen and started looking in pots for anything that hadn't been put away. I was dying for a cinnamon roll and told the cook hers were the best I'd had. Now we're great buddies. I go in after lunch, and they fix me a plate of the best leftovers. They said they'd save me a lunch if I wanted, but I get better choices this way. Sometimes, if I'm really late, the lead woman will call my office and see if I want something sent over. It's our secret because they don't want to do it for everyone. I have the best people I can find to supervise the cafeteria now.

Sometimes new APs build connections and reputations by intervening when the social hierarchy lines are crossed and teacher and noncertificated conflicts erupt in which the classified staff member is ill treated. One woman responsible for master schedule construction told us of her outrage when her secretary was abused by a teacher:

He came into the office, upset with me about a change in the schedule. When he couldn't get to see me right away, he became abusive to my secretary. He was yelling at her, blaming her for everything wrong in this school, and started giving her all kinds of orders. She was embarrassed and hurt and, of course, completely innocent. It all took place right out there in the hallway, with students and other adults hearing it all. When I heard about it, I was so angry that I went directly to his classroom and confronted him. I guess I was lucky that it was his preparation hour because I was really mad. I closed the door and told him we needed to get some things straightened out. He started yelling about his schedule, but I told him the issue right now was his treatment of my secretary. He dismissed it as if it were nothing, and I completely lost my temper and told him he could kiss his computers good-bye and start brushing up on his remedial math if he ever talked to her that way again.

Another, who became the AP for student activities, plant management, and discipline where he had taught and knew the teachers
well, told us a different kind of story:

> The most fun I've had this year was during the first week of
> this semester when one of our custodians who's been here for
> years came into my office and his face was as white as your
> shirt. He closed the door and said, "I have to talk to you. Did
> she call you?" I thought, oh God, what's happened now?
>
> I told him no one had called and to sit down. He said
> "Herself, the Queen Bee" [an English teacher] had called
> saying she needed more chairs and wanted him to bring her
> at least a half dozen right away. This is a big campus, and the
> chairs are stored clear across the campus, but there are always
> class size adjustments every semester and he knew teachers
> needed chairs. While he was loading these up, driving the cart
> across campus and carrying them up the stairs 'cause there's
> no elevator in that building and her class is on the second floor,
> she got impatient and went to another teacher's empty room
> and took some chairs. When the custodian got there, she said
> she didn't need the chairs anymore. She didn't tell him he
> could put them in the other teacher's room, let alone thank
> him for his work. She just told him to take them back. So he
> took them back.
>
> Two periods later, the other teacher got his new semester
> class. The class was bigger than he had expected, and he came
> and took his chairs back. So she called the custodian again. He
> dutifully brought more chairs back and lugged them up the
> stairs. He brought eight. She only needed five. He said he'd
> leave them there until all the classes were sorted out on that
> floor. She told him he couldn't leave them in her room. He
> said he couldn't leave them in the hall because of the fire
> regulations. She said she didn't care about that and ordered
> him to take the chairs back to storage. You must know her and
> know him to appreciate this. He is the most mild-mannered
> man you'd ever want to meet, and she is arrogant, unpleasant,
> critical, imperious. I could just see it when he told me. She
> pointed her finger at him and in her Queen Mother voice

pretty much told him to obey his betters. In a once-in-a-life-time response, he told her she could go fuck herself, turned, walked out, and left the chairs in her room.

He came right to my office, sure she was right on his heels or that she had already called. He thought he was in terrible trouble and that he'd be disciplined, maybe suspended or even fired. I couldn't help but laugh, and he didn't know what to think. I just couldn't stop. He was so scared. I told him to go hide out for a while, to come back in 2 hours, not to answer his phone until I saw him again, and not to tell anyone what had happened. I told him to relax a little. He had just done what most of the faculty members had wanted to do for a decade.

He left, and I decided I wasn't going to wait for her to come to the office. I went to the principal and told him what had happened. He was unofficially pleased. Then I went out to the English teacher's room. I thought I'd give her a chance to tell me what had happened, sort of meet the lion in her den. So I walked into her room. She had her class going. She gave me that "What do you want?" look, so I said I was just checking on how the first day of the semester was going and seeing if everyone had all the chairs they needed. She glared, but she didn't say anything. I'm sure she knew that I knew, but she hasn't yet said anything. I don't know what I would have done if she had—tried to make a joke of it, I guess. I love it! I laughed all the way back to the office. I did tell the custodian, though, to change some assignments and let someone else work that building for a while and not to press his luck too much. Now we joke about it every time I see him.

Sometimes, however, the best of relationships must yield to the realities of job responsibility, the contract, and the law. New APs find classified staff evaluation usually easier than teacher evaluation because so much more of what they do is visible and can be measured objectively. But incidents of malfeasance and problems of interpersonal relations are no less frustrating and unsettling. They confront laziness:

I was getting complaints from the coaches that the gym, the weight room, and the locker areas were not being cleaned and that equipment wasn't being secured. That's work shared by the night shift and the early morning custodians. We have a swing-shift crew from 3:30 to 11:30 and then another that works the graveyard. I decided to go in early one morning before they got off to talk to the guys working and to see what the situation was. I got to school a few minutes before 6:00 and worked my way through the maze in our gym without seeing anybody. When I went into the weight room, there was the custodian sound asleep on one of the padded benches. I couldn't believe it. Just flat out cold. I wanted to fire him, but our progressive discipline program wouldn't allow it. So now I'm documenting everything and we're in this contest. It's really frustrating.

And APs confront criminal activity like theft:

We had an operations worker stealing tools and supplies. I guess it's been going on quite a while. He had a terrible fight with the woman he was living with. She left him and called the principal and told him about all the stuff he had in the garage. Since I'm responsible for plant management and supervise the operations staff, it fell to me to go over to his house with the district director of maintenance and the police. His place was full of school stuff. He was arrested, and now we're in the process of firing him. Nobody ever said this kind of thing was going to be part of my job as an AP-slash-educational leader.

Learning to Work With a Secretary

Probably the most important relationship beginning APs have to establish is with their secretaries. For most, having a secretary is a novel experience and requires considerable adjustment. No AP we spoke with had ever had formal instruction about working with a secretary. For many new APs, the first few weeks or months with a secretary is a period of discovery and interpersonal adjustment. A man told us:

I found myself trying to impress her as much as anybody. She seemed to know so much about what was going on, it was intimidating. I was supposed to be the boss, but she was frequently telling me what I needed to attend to.

A woman outlined another kind of adjustment to be made:

We had completely different work styles at the outset. I guess she thought I would run this office like my predecessor did, and it didn't work. She wouldn't let people in without an appointment. She didn't screen the mail. She rewrote a lot of the things I wrote. At the same time, she always checked with me before she would give anyone an answer. I was interrupted with things I shouldn't have been bothered with. We had a lot of conflict. Well, it was more confusion than conflict, I guess, but it was a rough time for a while.

Sometimes a new AP will get lucky and have the pleasure of working with a secretary who understands what a newcomer is going through and needs:

The first thing she did when I was appointed, before I even came into the office, was to call me and suggest we get together. She wanted to tell me how the office ran right now and wanted to know how I liked to work. I didn't know how I liked to work. I'd never done this kind of work before. So she asked me if I wanted to do something this way or that way, giving me a choice and teaching me different ways at the same time. She never bad-mouthed the AP who was leaving; she just said things like, it would probably be easier for her to cover for me if I would tell her where I was going and when I would be back. She also has taught me a lot about the job itself: procedures, time lines, all the stuff that could get me into trouble.

To varying degrees, most of the new APs told us that they had received more help in learning their jobs from their secretaries, and often from other members of the classified staff, than they had anticipated and that some of it was crucial to their success. What amounts to an administrative staff development program seems to go unrecognized in many schools and districts, but building administrators know. In one district, an attendance office secretary is legend for her training of administrators. A superintendent, four principals, and seven APs then working in the district began their administrative careers working "for" her. Over the years, the attendance office had come to be known as "Betty M's School of Administration."

The Power of the Classified Staff

The informal power of classified staff members is a familiar phenomenon in most organizations and not unique to schools. The ability of lower ranking workers to sway decisions and affect behavior flows from the same source as official power: dependence. They have power to the extent that they can control or control access to information, people, materials, and services (Mechanic, 1962).

Secretaries often play a very important public relations role because of their regular contact with other schools and the community. Experienced secretaries also serve as a rich resource of information that is unavailable elsewhere because they tap into both the formal and informal organizations. They frequently have insider knowledge on how things are done, on shortcuts to securing materials and services, and on placing pending matters in context. Also, and very important, they may provide advice and warnings about particular preferences and sensitivities of other administrators, teachers, and parents. By applying their knowledge and employing their skills to the AP's benefit, they also demonstrate how much more difficult things might be if they withheld them. They can save new APs embarrassment and costly mistakes:

> California law requires a certain number of minutes of instruction spread over 180 days to meet state attendance and funding requirements. She read all the definitions and regulations and showed me that some of the time and activities we were counting didn't fit the state definitions. It sounds small, but it isn't. A district nearby was fined over $100,000 when the state audit showed they were under the minimum.

Sometimes they can make the difference between success and failure in public events:

> When we had the slowdown last fall, I don't know how she did it, but my secretary talked a half dozen of the clerks into filling in at the graduation. They stayed after and distributed and collected the caps and gowns and handed out the diplomas when the teachers who were scheduled to do it refused. We would have been in a real mess if they hadn't done it, and they did it only because she and the principal's secretary leaned on them.

Similar influence is exercised by members of the custodial and operations staff. New administrators who are responsible for registration, parent meetings, dances, athletic contests, graduations, school plays, and other activities learn quickly that the success of the event depends almost as much on the work of the operations staff as it does on the activity of the people who planned it. Equipment that does not arrive on time or is not set up properly, areas that are not cleaned as they should be, items that are not double-checked, or possible problems that are not communicated can tarnish or ruin any gathering or performance.

There are a hundred ways in which classified staff members can make new administrators more effective and efficient or just look good. There are a hundred more ways in which classified staff members can sabotage a new administrator's best efforts, and they do it simply by never saying a word and just letting events take their natural course. That is power, and the lesson to new administrators is that if they fail to establish strong working relationships with the support staff, they do so at their own peril.

New Perspectives and Relationships

Working With Other Administrators

> *A companion's words of persuasion are effective.*
> Homer, *The Iliad*

The young assistant principal sat in a cramped office that looked as if it had been a storage closet in a former life. A desk, file cabinet, bookcase, and two chairs were squeezed into a windowless space next to the attendance office. "They've all accepted me," he said, pointing to the other administrators' offices that punctuated the main hallway. "They've made me feel very, very welcome, more than the teachers' group did when I first became a teacher. And that was a very pleasant surprise. In fact, after my first week as an administrator, I went home and told my wife that I already felt like a part of the team."

The first-year APs we talked with consistently said they felt wanted and welcomed by their new colleagues. Because their stories take so many shapes, it is difficult to assess exactly why new assistants so commonly feel accepted and encouraged in their jobs. It may be because there are fewer administrators than teachers in a secondary school, and they are drawn together—or perhaps driven together—by the nature of the work. Perhaps it is because new administrators escape the isolation from other adults that marked their teaching experience, and that contrast alone is sufficient to foster feelings of companionship. It could be because the administrative group deliberately styles itself as a team and consciously works to integrate new members. Most likely, the reasons are different for each person.

Whatever the causes, research indicates that early acceptance of beginners is important, especially when someone is the only new hire at a given time, as are many new APs. Being the only newcomer to a team can be an unsettling experience. Socialization can take much longer because solitary recruits lack recourse to others sharing the same experience (Feldman & Arnold, 1983). Acceptance by the supervisor and peers, however, can compensate for the fact that the newcomer is alone.

The creation of an initial reference group is important for all first-year employees (Buchanan, 1974). Colleagues who welcome new members provide guidance and reassurance and offer opportunities for newcomers to earn respect and affection. In the process, coworkers exert a strong and perhaps lasting influence over the beginner's attitudes. In secondary schools, both the principal and peers play important roles in the socialization process.

The Influence of the Principal

As a beginner's first supervisor, the principal's efforts to clarify organizational culture and expectations simultaneously help reduce newcomer uncertainty and give the principal considerable influence. The exact nature and extent of the influence depends on a variety of organizational, cultural, and personal factors, but the new APs with whom we spoke confirmed research showing that the initial supervisor plays a very important role in a beginner's adjustment and development (e.g., Greenfield, 1985; Greenfield, Marshall, & Reed, 1986; Schein, 1987).

The new APs reported general satisfaction with the support they received from their principals, but they frequently were surprised to discover the style diversity that exists among effective principals. Some discovered that the principals for whom they worked (and they used *for* more than *with*) differed markedly from the ideal models they had studied in their preparation programs. New assistants seem to discover through the unfolding of daily events that a principal is competent or more than competent without reference to a particular theory or model. As one junior high AP told us:

> It's been an adjustment for me. This principal is so different from the principal of my last school, so fixed on instruction. The principal I worked for before pretty much let teachers do their own thing. Here, there is a straight-line connection between what teachers are taught in the workshops, what she looks for and has me look for in teacher observations, and what goes into the teacher's evaluation and goals for next year. She knows what she wants and so do the teachers, and they respond. Everybody tells me this is a better school than it was a few years ago, before she came. Just between you and me, though, I'm glad I came here as an administrator and not as a teacher. I'm not sure I could take the close supervision.

An AP from another junior high told a different story:

> The principal here is really good. He can tell you what we're about, and he's willing to let the teachers find their own ways to get to the goals. His single rule of evaluation is simple: Does whatever we're talking about get us closer to the goal we've set? If the answer is yes, he supports it. If not, he doesn't.
>
> I don't think the principal knows very much about curriculum or instruction, but [the AP assigned to oversee it] sure does. She and I do almost all the teacher observation. The principal is out in rooms a lot, but he doesn't really observe what is going on. He is very smooth, though. Somehow the teachers always have the equipment and materials they want. He got parents to build a new greenhouse for the Science Department, and the students also grow plants there to plant around the school.

Many new APs are surprised by discrepancies between what principals say and do. Some are initially put off by the differences between what Argyris and Schon (1974) call principals' "espoused" theories—what they say they believe—and "theories-in-action"—what they do that demonstrates what they actually believe. A high school AP provided a telling example:

> He does the same thing with us as he does with the teachers. He says we're all really talented and he wants to know what we think, but he does most of the talking every time we get together. He says we're empowered, but what we're really empowered to do is what he wants us to do.

Other APs discover the gap between the principal's espoused philosophy and actual behavior in day-to-day revelations coming from small and relatively isolated incidents. For example, many new assistants are surprised when the principal modifies or even reverses a disciplinary decision. Others are surprised when they learn that the principal has overridden a decision they made in response to a teacher's request. These are lessons of organizational priority and power that at first are difficult for some new APs to understand and accept.

Learning to work with administrators who do not match textbook descriptions of ideal leaders can be a challenge, but the experience can broaden new APs' definitions of what constitutes "good" administration. Research reveals that leading a secondary school is a complex undertaking and that there is no one best way. The literature contains interesting and varied descriptions of successful principals, ranging from dynamic people who orchestrate nearly everything to those whose great talents lie in selecting strong faculty members and delegating authority (Wilson & Corcoran, 1988). Rather than consistent, open, "company" people who believe themselves limited by their job descriptions and allotted authority, principals are often politicians and influence wielders (Cuban, 1986; Duane, Bridgeland, & Stern, 1986; Ubben & Hughes, 1992). The range of their behavior is not confined to the patterns that dominate the prescriptive literature today. One study found four effective high school principals who had no preconceived "vision" as they led their schools (Keedy, 1991). Instead, they "scanned" the environments of their buildings, developing and adjusting their ideas of what ought to be as they went along, opportunistically searching for anything to improve their schools.

Behavioral inconsistencies cause many new APs to revise their original estimations of their principals as educational leaders. Nevertheless, the new APs with whom we spoke reported, almost without exception, feeling that the principal was glad to have them on the staff and was interested in seeing them succeed. A former mathematics teacher now responsible for curriculum and instruction, student teachers, and discipline put it this way:

> There's a lot the principal and I don't agree on, but she has been wonderful to me personally. From the minute I was selected, she started asking what she could do to help me. We had several meetings before school started, just as soon as I moved here, and talked about the strengths and weaknesses of this school and the people in it. She was very open with me and made it very clear that she expected me to concentrate on improving articulation with our feeder schools this year. For me, though, the best thing she's done is limit some of my projects. I have a friend at another school who's going in six directions at once.

A woman who oversaw guidance, student activities, and discipline described her experience:

> I'll tell you what he did, and I didn't really realize it until about May, when one of the other APs pointed it out to me. The principal came into my office a lot during the first semester just to visit. I was afraid at first that he was checking up on me or didn't trust me, but that wasn't it. Whenever there was a problem, he'd call me to his office, but he never brought a problem to mine that I can remember. He just came to see how I was doing. He'd shut the door and ask how it was going and what I thought. Then he'd tell me about how much he'd enjoyed being an AP and all the things he'd learned, which are the same things I'm learning.

Sometimes we heard stories that, judging by the relish with which they were told, suggested that the principal would have a strong influence on how a new AP ultimately defined himself or herself as an administrator. A man responsible for curriculum and instruction, records, discipline, and teacher supervision provided a good example:

> Have I ever been surprised by the principal's behavior? You don't know! He is something. I was sitting in his office one morning, not really doing anything, just talking. All at once, this man bursts into the office. Fancy suit, red in the face, obviously angry. It startled the principal and me. He had just brushed by the secretary and charged right in. He never even looked at me. He just stood across the desk from the principal and said, in a real loud voice, almost yelling, "I want to see you! I'm so-and-so's father and I'm an attorney."
>
> The principal didn't do anything, didn't get up, didn't even move. Then, in a real calm voice, he said, "And I like Mexican food." The man just exploded: "What in the god-damned hell has that got to do with anything?" Then the principal stood up, leaned across the desk and said, "About as much as you being an attorney. Now listen, you son-of-a-bitch. If you want to come in here and tell me you're an attorney, then put your ass in that chair while I call our attorney, 'cause I won't spend 30 seconds of my time on you. That intimidation crap isn't going to work here. But if you want to come in here as so-and-so's father to talk to so-and-so's principal so we can work together to solve whatever the problem is, sit down and we'll visit. That's what I'm here for. Now, what do you want to do?"
>
> I thought, oh, Christ, this is going to be something. There were a couple of what they call "pregnant seconds," then you could just see the man deflate. He apologized and sat down and said he'd like to talk with the principal about some problem his son was having with a teacher. The principal looked at me, asked if I would excuse them, and I left. The principal's secretary told me an hour later that they came out of the office, laughing like they were old school chums and everything was just fine. I don't think I'll ever forget that!

Organizations socialize their new members through experiences that serve to undo old values so that the newcomer will be prepared to learn new ones (Schein, 1987). Some of these experiences result from planned activities such as orientations, team-building retreats, workshops, and the assignment of specific tasks with directions to accomplish them in certain ways; others flow from day-to-day organizational life and the beginner's observation of how priorities are established, decisions made, and conflicts resolved. The messages contained in these experiences are often surprising, sometimes disturbing, and occasionally painful, but the guidelines that superiors and senior members provide in one fashion or another are among the most potent sources of learning for newcomers (Schein, 1987).

The Influence of Peers

As powerful as the principal is in the socialization of new administrators, first-year APs also are shaped by what they learn from other assistants. People new to a job are anxious to show their peers, as well as their superiors, that they can adjust to situations and learn what is needed to be successful (Wheeler, 1966). This anxiety leads them to pay close attention to their work partners' attitudes and behaviors. Newcomers look to members in their immediate work groups for clues on deciphering the new setting (D. C. Fisher, 1986; Latane, 1981; Schein, 1987). As a result, they are vulnerable to their colleagues' influence. Research clearly shows that peers play important roles in helping newcomers feel at home and become effective (Latane, 1981; Louis, Posner, & Powell, 1983). In schools large enough to have two or more APs, peers are important sources of organizational learning. As one man, a former English teacher, told us:

I was having a terrible time getting the district crews to come work on our fields. We have a lot of community use after hours and on weekends, and our fields got torn up over the summer. We needed resodding and a lot of other work to be ready for the fall. I put in work order after work order, and nothing happened. I put together a report that detailed every need and chronicled every order and follow-up call I had put through. I was really frustrated with the whole system. I asked one of the other APs to proof it for me before I sent it off to the director of maintenance. She asked me if the principal knew about this. I said he didn't. I wanted to show that I could get things done without whining to him for help. She said that was good, but I'd better tell him what I was doing. He'd probably approve it, but he doesn't want anything going to the district office that he doesn't know about in advance. She said he'd hang me right out if the district called about some report or complaint that he wasn't aware of.

Another man, also coming straight from the classroom, offered this example:

I'm learning a lot from [the female AP]. She has an attitude that's wonderful. I was dreading discipline, and I was right about that for a lot of it, but she keeps telling me that some of it can really be fun if you think about it in certain ways. She sees it simultaneously as a game and as a great counseling activity. I don't think she ever just assigns someone detention or a work detail, let alone suspends them or even has them arrested, without really making an effort to talk with them and shape their attitudes. Discipline is teaching, she says.

But she does things I'd never think of doing. We have a closed campus, but this place is so wide open that kids can get out of here at lunch without much trouble at all. When the new McDonald's opened up in October, we started having kids zip up there in their cars and get hamburgers. We tried all kinds of things, like having a monitor at the parking lot gate, but there are just too many kids who leave legitimately, and it takes too long to check passes on every student leaving the campus. The three of us [APs] would go up to McDonald's, but the place is almost all glass, and they'd see us coming and split. Then one day she came in and said, "I've got it." She went up to McDonald's an hour before lunch, put on one of their smocks and caps and went to work in the drive-through window. When a carload of kids came through with one of our parking stickers, she'd take their order, tell them it would be

$5.00 or something at the window, and to drive forward. When they'd get to the window, she'd say, "Here's your Big Mac, fries, and a shake—and here's your detention slip. Be in my office when I get back." It was wonderful.

Other APs talked with us about how their peers handle irate parents, calm tense situations with teachers and students, solve technical problems, and find humor in the most serious of situations. One man told us about the "office trophy," a plaster-of-paris hand giving the finger, which is awarded each week to the AP who puts on the best performance with a student or parent. The winner gets to keep it, undisplayed of course, in his or her office until the next cabinet meeting.

For most of the new APs in our groups, the opportunity to socialize with other administrators outside work was a surprise. Many had experienced a social distance between administrators and teachers in the schools where they had taught. This socializing was important for them, increasing both their comfort level and strengthening their ties to the organization.

Of course, not all new APs find other administrators to be as friendly or positive as they had hoped or expected. Why does one long-term AP remain positive and effective and another become disenchanted and cynical? Answers vary.

Many career APs maintain their positive views of schools and students over decades (Marshall, 1993), whereas others facing similar challenges succumb to negativity as a result of ingrained personality traits or aspects of the job. Thwarted career aspirations can stir negativity in some. Most APs regard the assistantship as a stepping stone to higher office, a place where they must "pay their dues" (Austin & Brown, 1970; Marshall, 1992, 1993). At the same time, the simple fact is that there are far more assistantships than principalships and that not every AP who aspires to will become a principal. For others, negativity may develop gradually from the confrontational nature of the work, especially discipline. This possibility is glimpsed in some of the APs' experiences reported in Chapter 4. It is important to note here that some experienced administrators' negativity may appear exaggerated to beginners because of the contrast between the newcomer's idealism and the veteran's realism.

An assistant responsible for student activities and discipline considered the contrast between herself and the veteran AP who ran the Guidance Office:

> She constructs the master schedule. I think she likes the technical challenge of making everything fit and solving the conflicts. She just loves the master schedule; it's like a living thing to her. She can massage it and manipulate it and make it do what she wants. But she punishes people with it. The conflict matrix printout is like a club in her hands. She discounts any arguments she gets from teachers that kids do better in certain subjects at certain times of day. The teachers are all the same to her, and that's the way she refers to them: "the teachers." She sees them as a monolithic block. And she has no patience for students and parents who don't immediately accept that a class has to be moved or canceled. She's convinced they've all been spoiled and that the principal is too weak to stand up to them.

The new APs with whom we spoke consistently reported concern, impatience, and distaste for the negativity they encountered but rarely indicated that they were targets of it. Thwarted veterans might be expected to resent talented beginners who are likely to reach the goals they never could; no doubt that happens, but apparently not particularly often. Many new APs were surprised to find that their colleagues gave them less direct assistance than they had hoped for, but very few suggested that anyone deliberately created problems for them.

One AP summed up the thoughts of many when she told us:

> I understand why he's never become a principal. He's just there. He does his own job well enough, but he doesn't go out of his way to help anyone else. I do think our principal would get rid of him if he could, but he was here before the principal came. He knows every attendance law there is, but he doesn't see any connection between attendance and counseling. We went to a conference at a resort hotel. I think all he did was sign in, go to the pool, and sign out. I never saw him in a session. He thinks a lot of education is just hooey.

Whether the association with peers is positive or negative, the new APs who talked with us drew lessons from their interactions in a fashion much like what Stohl (1986) calls "memorable messages." Certain ideas and values are picked up by beginners early in their socialization to a new career. These notions then stay with them, guiding their behavior, often for decades, as "personalized proverbs." These do not appear in writing anywhere, certainly not in any official organizational literature. Teachers have their set—for example, "Never smile until after Thanksgiving," "Never challenge the principal in an open meeting," and "Never trust the administration." New administrators learn their own.

Typical messages received by the new APs we talked with included "Parents want you to discipline everyone else's children," "Never trust an old enemy or a new friend," "Always double-check meeting arrangements yourself," "The Board will always back down to parents," "Secretaries always know what's going on," "Never get your honey where you get your money," "There are no secrets in schools," and "The principal isn't always right, but he's always the principal." One new AP had been convinced that "sooner or later, any boy named Jason will be a discipline problem," but no one else confirmed it. It is impossible to know which "message," if any, will prove "memorable," but their impact on beginning APs is important.

Memorable messages are important because newcomers need help in making sense of their surroundings and in interpreting the events in which they take part (Louis, 1980). Because the environment is new and they have not yet had time to internalize organizational values and operating norms, novices have heightened sensitivity and need explanatory devices. Identical experiences and explanations given 2 or 3 years later are not likely to have the impact they have during the first year or to be perceived as insightful or even important. The messages may seem clichéd and trite to an outsider, but they are highly meaningful to someone searching for understanding (Weick, 1979).

Peers help new APs make sense of their responsibilities and relationships through mentoring, memorable messages, explanations, deliberate demonstrations, and even bad examples. Newcomers also gain valuable organizational knowledge simply by observing how their peers operate. This knowledge is important because, at the outset, the manner in which insiders and beginners interpret their experiences may differ significantly (Louis, 1980). Insiders more often know what to expect in a situation and what will grow out of it. They can place even surprising events in the context of the organization and its population. Their history provides them with the relevant information they need to see ramifications and implications. Beginners cannot draw on such a history. A close relationship with peers helps new APs more quickly understand their new positions and the events they encounter.

The Impact of the Job

Opinion is ultimately determined by the feelings, and not by the intellect.

Spenser, *Social Statics*

The assistant principal's window looked out on a flagpole surrounded by a patch of well-kept grass where students sat in groups of six or seven eating lunch. As she talked with us, she checked the window every few minutes, sweeping her eyes expertly over the area for any signs of trouble. The poster behind her desk showed a road stretching in a limitless line into the Arizona desert. The quotation under it read: "You always have two ways to run. Away from . . . or towards." She turned back to face us. "You want to know if this job has changed me?" She smiled, thought for a minute. "Yeah, I've changed, and I think for the better. There are times when I feel incredibly insecure and anxious, but overall, I know I'm more confident. After 6 months here, I'm beginning to feel like an assistant principal."

Virtually all of the new APs with whom we spoke told us that the job affects them more than any other school job they ever held. After

124

all, in a short time, they had to alter long-held perspectives on schools, enter a new peer group, redefine relations with former colleagues, and establish working associations with a new group of subordinates, while taking on unfamiliar, multiple, rapidly paced, and sometimes highly emotional tasks. Some see the changes as trying and distressing, others as energizing signs of growth and increased capacity. Either way, the changes require adjustment.

The impact of becoming an AP on any given individual is impossible to predict. The variables are too many and a single year is too short to determine whether new attitudes and behaviors are manifestations of profound change or just a phase of adjustment. The first year in a new position produces both permanent and passing shifts in emotion, attitude, and behavior (Berlew & Hall, 1966; Brett, 1984; Feldman, 1989; C. D. Fisher, 1986; Louis, 1980; Nicholson & West, 1988). What is certain is that every new AP somehow feels the effects of the job.

This impact is felt in three ways, each with distinctly unlimited personal versions. First, other people have an impact on new APs, who often are surprised, even overwhelmed, by how involved they become in the lives of those with whom they interact, students and adults alike. Second, the needs of the organization itself—the bureaucracy, technical requirements, and legalities—burden newcomers with a heavy weight of complicated tasks and time-consuming responsibilities. Third, the job affects the emotions of new APs, both positively and negatively. Many express anger and frustration about situations they are unable to control or resolve; some fear for their personal safety. Others enjoy the pace, finding the action exhilarating and renewing. Many revel in the new, satisfying feeling of being at the hub of the school. Some describe an array of negative specifics but conclude that the overall changes in themselves are positive; others describe the reverse. The impact of the job is as individual as it is unavoidable.

Interpersonal Impact

Many new APs are surprised by the intensity of their interactions with the lives of other people on the job. Because the heart of the job is conflict resolution, APs are called on daily to untangle multi-layered issues that often involve a complex web of relationships. No wonder, then, that a common theme in the stories we were told centered on an inability to leave problems at work at the end of the day. As one man told us:

> I have been surprised by how much I take home. I didn't think I would get as involved with the problems of these kids like I do, or with some of the relations with teachers, but I do. *There* was a big change, a big surprise in my home life. I've never been one to take the job home with me. It might eat at me inside, but I don't discuss it much. Now I'm starting to. Luckily for me, I've been married to the same person for 24 years. If we had been married less time, I don't know . . .

Part of the reason new assistants mentally take work home with them stems from the pace of the job. The flow of events and the decision-press at school are so hectic that new APs often engage in a sort of situational triage. Items that absolutely cannot be completed or resolved at the moment are put aside in favor of those that must be handled immediately. Later, at home, these items, which still require attention, bubble to the surface. Many new assistants told us they keep notepads by their beds to record thoughts or ideas that wake them in the night. It is very difficult for many new APs to turn off their attention to school matters just because they are away from school.

Much more than the sheer number, the emotional intensity of some incidents causes troubled, preoccupied hours at home. Although few interactions actually have this effect, many new APs are affected deeply enough by them to feel themselves continually bombarded. Whether it is because of the general uncertainty they feel about their jobs (Louis, 1980) or the contrast with the kinds of problems they used to deal with in the classroom, many new APs are regularly disturbed by what they encounter.

Nagging involvements occur in virtually every facet of a new assistant's interactions, but the strongest are often those that involve the welfare of their coworkers. One man in a middle school told us about the burden of confidential information:

Someone comes to you with questions about someone else's behavior and you know answers, but you can't tell 'em. I had a teacher come in to conference with me, and we drifted off teaching and into personal things. All at once, he's in tears and telling me that he knew his wife was having an affair with another teacher on this campus, and it was tearing him up. He must have sobbed for 5 minutes. I did the best I could for him, but there really wasn't anything for me to do. But I can't stop thinking about it. I wonder who the other teacher is, and I feel for the man in my office. Later, his department chair came in to complain about this man's uncooperative attitude and the complaints coming in about his teaching. What am I supposed to do? I stare at the bedroom ceiling thinking about it.

Another woman told us about her first year's experience in teacher evaluation and her feelings about doing what she knows needs to be done about a poor teacher:

I feel bad about it, and it keeps me awake sometimes. There's a teacher here, he's in his 40s, and he's been teaching for more than 20 years. The principal's been here 2 years longer than I have and has had one problem after another with him: He doesn't have any classroom control; he's boring; he sends kids to the office all the time; he acts strangely. Parents don't just complain, they try to take preemptive strikes. They call up months in advance to keep their kids from being scheduled into his classes.

The principal assigned me right after the holidays to observing him all the time, formal and drop-ins, documenting every discipline incident, going back and analyzing the records for attendance in his classes, grade distributions, transfers out, all that sort of stuff. The man really is a poor teacher. I hate the conferences after the observations. I have to tell him bad news every time. He gets upset; I get upset. And nothing changes.

I know he can't be left in the classroom where he is. It's not fair to the students. He's an awful teacher, but I think he's a good man. I mean, he introduced me to his wife and kids at the back-to-school faculty picnic in August. They're really nice people. I know he's active in his church, from what other teachers have told me. He brought in all kinds of stuff for the needy during the Salvation Army drive. He comes to every football and basketball game. He and his wife were at the play 2 weeks ago. He's a lousy teacher, but he's a good husband and father, I think. I feel like I'm part of something that can ruin his life. It bothers me. I didn't bargain for this.

Nor are the situations limited to the certificated staff. An AP in a large high school told us about reacting to problems one of the custodians was having:

I got a call that one of the custodians was holed up in one of the rest rooms and wouldn't come out. His supervisor told me that he was acting very strangely and had been depressed for quite a while. He'd tried to get him to contact the Employee Assistance Office, but he'd never do it. I have pretty good rapport with this custodian because my office is on his work list. I went out to the rest room with another AP to talk to him. To make a long story short, I got him to open up for me. He looked terrible. Then he broke down into tears and said he wanted help. It ended up that the other AP and I took him to the emergency room at County Hospital. They're so backed up there, they asked us to take him up to the psychiatric unit on the fifth floor. So we did. I've never been anywhere like that before. It was indescribable. We had to leave him there.

New APs also are drawn into the lives of students. Working in discipline and student activities often creates close ties, opening up the private lives of students. A man in a high school told us about his Student Council members:

I didn't expect to, but I've really become close to the 12 kids I work with in the [ASB] cabinet. We do things, like miniature golf or go bowling. We go somewhere, and then I take them home afterward, and I see where some of them stay at night and the home situation. I've become more reflective, more thankful for the things that I have because of what I've seen in this situation in terms of economic level in the area.

You know, we'll sit in the office and talk about going out for pizza Friday night after the game, and they'll say, "Yeah! yeah!" Well, when we get there and start ordering pizzas, some will say, "I'm not hungry. I don't want any." You know what the bottom line is? They don't have any money to help pay. And that is frustrating to me because then I feel like, well, I'll buy it. And then my wife says, "Are you going to pay for them every time you go out? You know, they have to learn you can't go out every time if you don't have any money." That's emotionally hard.

Discipline often causes emotional reactions, as illustrated in Chapter 4. New APs can get very involved when the plight of students is particularly serious and they know the parents:

I had this boy so stuck on drugs who was just hard core. The police brought him in a couple of times when they picked him up truant. It was always from near the same place, a garage in the next block. They were sure he had drugs, but they couldn't ever catch him with any. Another AP and I were out on a truancy sweep one day during lunch and saw him. He didn't go to the garage. Instead, he went between two houses and hunkered down behind a bush. [The other AP] went around and came in from the back, and I came in from the front. He was sniffing cocaine when we came on him. He is the son of one of our teachers here. It was terrible. There was a scene, first between the boy and his father, and then his father wanted me to bend the rules for him. I wanted to more than anything, but I couldn't. Now we have a very strained relationship.

For a few APs, those whose children attend the school where they work, escape can be impossible. Even when they are able to set aside their work burdens at the end of the day, the school meets them at home for dinner:

I see 2,000 teenagers a day. Then I go home and there are 2 more! I have two kids in the school, a senior daughter and a freshman son. Between them, they seem to know every time I bust someone. It's dinner table conversation. Sometimes it'll get tense because I can tell they know something more than I do, but they won't tell me. They get upset if I don't share all I know; they think I don't trust them—which I can't. Worse, though, my wife gets upset with talk about drugs and thefts and fights and teachers. We almost have to call a truce sometimes.

Another unique danger is inherent in being responsible for discipline where your own children attend school:

My elder son is a junior at our school. He got crossways of a teacher, and I had to suspend him. He was just dead wrong. He was mad, but we got it settled. I suspended him for 2 days, just like I would anyone else, and he understood it. As he was going out the door, though, I told him that the suspension paid his debt to the school—but just wait until his father got home! Fortunately, his sin was just teenage foolishness. It scares me to death to think what would happen if he was involved in something serious like drugs or weapons.

For most new APs, the ultimate emotional burdens are linked to student death. Most first-year assistants probably will not have to face such a loss, but some do, and it is a wrenching experience. Perhaps the most dramatic example we had came from a first-year AP in a "good school," a 9th- through 12th-grade high school with an enrollment under 1,000, where the students come from mixed socioeconomic backgrounds—some relatively affluent, some poor. The 15% non-White population is a mixture of Asian, African American, Samoan, and Hispanic students. This is not what anyone would consider a troubled inner-city school, but these days schools everywhere are vulnerable to violence and death. During this AP's first year, two students committed suicide, one was killed by police, one was murdered, one died from alcohol poisoning, and one was killed in a random gang shooting. Although this is far from a typical school year, it illustrates the kinds of turmoil and tragedy that can erupt anywhere.

Organizational Impact

Pale in comparison with the human problems, but frequent and real nonetheless, are problems new assistants experience with the technical complexities of their work. Almost every one of the APs with responsibility for creating the master schedule, for example, told us that, at some point, usually the last few days before the beginning of the semester, they become obsessed by it. So much rides on what they do.

In other offices, other APs share similar feelings about attendance accounting because these duties mean money gained or lost. Some worry about budget errors or staffing ratios. One assistant had a major responsibility in preparing the school's accreditation report and not only continually worked on it at home but also had trouble sleeping until it was done.

Still other new APs wrestle with legal questions: new hire background checks, marginal employee documentation, wrongful discharge lawsuit threats, the intricacies of special education law, civil rights violations in search and seizure, technicalities of arrest or expulsion procedures, and charges of censorship or discrimination. They know the media are always out there. They can easily picture themselves in the midst of bad publicity that can ruin a school's reputation, and maybe their own. One high school AP responsible for the prom related that a homosexual couple planned to attend, which violated school policy and stirred considerable controversy. The prom was still the better part of a month away, but he had been contacted by the ACLU declaring an intention to litigate, which had considerably "rattled" him, as he put it. He had not been prepared for this kind of confrontation in his university work nor envisioned seeing his name in the newspaper in connection with this aspect of school life.

Legal concerns weigh heavily in the thinking of many new APs. Litigation seems always just a step away, and fears of negligence are so pervasive in schools that they sometimes alter an assistant's perspective in disturbing ways. A man responsible for athletic administration provided an unsettling example:

> I had just gotten home from a meeting when I got a phone call that a sophomore boy had just collapsed during practice and died on the track. He was running sprints, and all at once he went down. The coach did the right thing: He immediately sent someone to call 911. But the boy died. I knew him just slightly. He was no great athlete, but he was a nice enough kid. I feel awful to tell you this, though: My first thought wasn't for him. My first reaction was, "Oh, God, did we screw up on his physical?" I sent the person who called me to pull the boy's file right away and see if we had all the health checks and permission slips we were supposed to have. It's bothered me a lot since then that that was my first thought. Even at the funeral, I was asking myself if his parents were going to sue us when this was over. It shouldn't be that way.

Emotional Impact

The emotional impact of the job is undeniable; every AP we talked with described a roller coaster of feelings throughout the first year. The emotional intensity is reflected in stories from new APs who told us they had more disturbing dreams about this job than they could remember having had about any other:

> I have nightmares about the job. There hasn't been one dream since September—no, even before that—where things have gone right for me. I've always left something undone or someone is mad at me or I'm at a board meeting and they ask me something I don't know anything about and I'm embarrassed to death. The only dream I haven't had yet is going to work naked, but I'll bet I'll have it before the year is over. Say, can you cause dreams by saying things like that?

Whether it disturbs their sleep or not, the job frustrates many new APs perhaps because they do not immediately attain the level of success they had expected. For most, this feeling eases with experience; many felt better about their level of control as they neared the end of the spring semester. At the outset, however, many new APs miss the control they had in the classroom, and they are surprised to feel, as one put it, "not like an administrator able to give orders, but like a teacher out of place." One man twiddled his tie and told us:

> I feel like this is the Oliver Hardy School of Administration: Well, here's another fine mess you've gotten me into! Except that I got myself into this mess. I always knew what I was doing in the classroom. Here . . .

Most APs are selected because of their efficacy in the classroom, so this new sense of incompetence is particularly painful. Said one woman, pointing to budget printouts:

> I'm not accustomed to this feeling. I'm used to plowing into something and mastering it. I'm not used to looking at something and not being able to decipher it.

The most powerful feelings new APs shared with us came from perceived threats of violence. Over the years, discipline administration has been a difficult part of the job for many assistants, but the relatively recent escalation of violence in and around schools has had a clear impact on the feelings of those now coming into the position. In many instances, they are afraid, and confronting their fear has become a daily part of the job. A new AP in an affluent area expressed it this way:

> I've had my window shot out twice now, and I've only been here, what, 3 months? 4 months? The AP in here before me was here for 15 years, and that happened only once to him in all that time. People come by and say, "Oh, you must be doing a good job," but I don't know. I don't feel like I'm an authoritarian crushing the kids. I try to deal with them humanely, try to make them realize we all have prices to pay for actions that we do. You know, if you want to spend a day at the beach, you're going to spend a day with us on Saturday, and that's

the choice you made. I have a lot of kids thank me as they leave the office; they're not mad. And then my windows get shot out! Every day, I sit in my office and think, Will it happen today?

A woman who would never say it aloud in a group told one of us privately:

I don't think I'd want to admit this to anybody, so I'll only say it here that I'm surprised at how insecure and frightened I feel at times. You know, if I let myself think about it, it gets overwhelming. I had no anticipation that I'd feel this way. Then I just remind myself, well, you like challenges. [laughs] Still, it makes me uneasy to walk into a group of kids and confront them. You never know.

Many new APs worry about the escalating threat of gangs. This comment was typical:

It's the kind of having to put your life on the line that we went through toward the beginning of school that is disturbing. We had a drive-by shooting. It was off campus, but it involved our kids, so we were on alert for retaliation. All the administrators were patrolling the perimeter, looking for suspicious cars, and all you're thinking about is if somebody's driving by, what are they going to aim for? I never expected that kind of thing. We joked about it, about issuing flak jackets, but still, when you come down to it, it's scary.

Sometimes the effects of the fear last beyond the workday:

I've never worried about being shot at before or felt daily concern for my personal safety. I student-taught in a tough school. I taught at [name] High School in the inner city. I've coached and been in bizarre places, and I never worried about it. But now it feels different. I was at dinner with a friend, and we walked into an alley, and I don't know what happened; I was real jittery and jumpy, and she said, "What is it?" and I said, "You know, I've gotten to the point where I'm always looking in every direction."

Because so much of what APs do involves conflict of one variety or another, many of their actions engender strong responses from faculty and staff members. These reactions often spark counter-responses. Many new APs are surprised at the intensity of the anger they feel toward others and sometimes discover a strength of temper they did not know they had, or at least a temper they were able to keep under control in other circumstances. For some, anger shows itself more with students; for others, with employees; for some, with parents. One high school assistant found his limits with a new student:

> I don't have any patience with that kind of thing. A boy moved here from out of state. He's the original redneck bigot! I'll bet he has a sheet and hood in his closet. I just lost it with him the other day. I was screaming at him about how he can't do the things he does to people who are different from him, at least not in this school. I really thought I was going to hit him. He just sat there and looked at me like he knew a secret—that I was the one who wasn't very bright. My secretary and the other AP came in when they heard the yelling. I calmed down on the surface, and the other AP took over, but it took me more than an hour to really get control again. I had to go out walking. That white trash son-of-a-bitch is going to kill some-one or get killed, and he won't listen to anything you try to tell him.

Another exploded at a teacher:

> This teacher is absolutely unreasonable. He is paranoid about his tests; he's sure someone's cheating every time he gives one. He doesn't want to let anyone take a makeup because he knows for sure that other kids will have told the absent student what's on it. He's forced by law to let legally absent students make up exams, so now he's started capping what you can get. There's no makeup grade above a C. Then he

locks students out if they're late, won't answer the door when they knock. He selectively enforces rules to the exact letter. A student coming in on a legitimate pass from his counselor or another teacher or even me can't get into class. If he finally does let him in, he's still counted as absent for the day and loses whatever points are awarded for attendance and participation.

We finally had it out. He pulled that shit on a kid I'd been working with who had a terrible situation at home. He was dying in most of his classes. One of his teachers sent him in for sleeping in class. I spent an hour and a half with him. I did some really good counseling, I thought—worked out some arrangements with the nurse and the cafeteria supervisor to give him some extra attention and got his first-period teacher to let me know right away if he wasn't there or if there seemed to be any kind of problem.

When I sent him to class, he was seeming pretty "up," and I was feeling pretty good. Then that bastard sends him back; wouldn't let him into class; bawled him out—at least not in the room like he usually does—out in the hall, but loud, and every kid in that class and the ones around it could hear the dressing down. I was so mad! I went right out to his room and knocked on the door. When he wouldn't answer, I unlocked it with my key and told him to come outside. Then I let him have it. I guess I did the same thing to him that he did to this boy, but I didn't care. The principal got on me later about the way I handled it, but it's not right. No one should treat kids that way. All that work, and this boy is so fragile, and [the teacher] can do that kind of damage with his tongue and his attitude. I'm not going to have it, that's all.

Anger over someone else's recalcitrance, prejudice, or abusiveness, even if it is handled in a manner less than professionally ideal, is understandable. Some new APs, however, believe that they are more susceptible to anger than they expected because they are so invested in what they do that, despite their best efforts, they sometimes take things more personally than they should. An attendance office AP was representative:

I had sort of told myself that I wasn't going to let things become personal. You know, that when teachers come in and unload both barrels, griping, that I knew it wasn't about me per se. They're not angry at me; they're angry at the system, or the situation, or what have you. And then one of the biggest mistakes I thought that administrators made was to be so defensive and to take things so personally. And I've been very surprised at how easily you can become defensive. [laughs]

You just take ownership of things. For instance, our first 4 months' attendance reports are horrible. We're at the bottom of the district. And nobody's saying anything to me, but I'm surprised at how bad that's making me feel and how irritated I am about the whole thing. I'm not personally doing anything that's so awful and shouldn't be so defensive about it. But it's so hard not to be; it's hard not to take it personally.

Sometimes the accumulated emotional burdens are too great, and new APs have second thoughts about pursuing an administrative career. Early job experiences shake their confidence in education, convincing some that the system is fundamentally flawed and cannot be made right and that the personal price it extracts is simply too high. These feelings are manifested in different ways:

I'm not as service oriented as I was at the beginning. There are too many students and teachers who won't take responsibility, who won't do what they should. I can't change them, and I'm not going to exhaust myself fighting with people for the opportunity to do them a favor. I'll go another year, but if it's not better then, I'm gone. I can do more good in the classroom without destroying myself.

Another echoed the feeling:

It never ends. These seniors will graduate, but three quarters of these kids will be back next year, along with a new freshman class, and it'll be more of the same. And it's the same with the teachers. I don't think you can change a lousy teacher. They laugh at you. They have tenure; I don't. I have tenure as a teacher, but not as an administrator. We don't make a lot of progress. A kid grows if he doesn't ruin himself with drugs, but a lot of teachers are done growing. What I do doesn't really make much difference.

Thoughts like these oppress many new APs, both at work and at home. Some become moody, discovering they give less not only at work but also at home. One man expressed it this way:

I have two sons. For them to make demands on my time after a very long and frustrating week is very hard to take and very difficult for them to understand. This is a surprise because I used to see administrators in my former district on weekends express some of what I'm saying now. I don't want my family to start seeming like an obligation.

On emotional overload at work, some new APs come home to find that the job is having a negative impact on their marriages. One man offered the following:

My wife doesn't really understand. I talk so much at work, I don't want to talk at home. I catch myself just going "um-hum" with her. My wife is a homemaker. Contrast her day with mine.

Another man talked about tuning out his wife by tuning in to television:

Some nights, I'll be a zombie sitting in front of the TV, and I don't even like TV. This is the fourth night in a row I've just zoned out in front of it. I almost feel like I need a hobby at home to release myself. Just talking isn't enough. I don't want to hear about my wife's day at her work. It just makes me compare hers to mine, and then I'm in the swamp again.

Another was trying to find a way to repair the damage done at home, even if it meant quitting the job:

I'd come home a tyrant, and I'd be tired. I talk to myself a lot now, convincing myself that it's okay, I've done all that I can do. I'm not going to come home and be dissatisfied or start putting all my thoughts into what I've done or didn't do that day. I've mellowed a little in that sense. It wasn't just taking its toll on me; it was taking it on our family. Probably the roughest time of my life has been these last 4, 5 months, to the point where I am thinking I'm going to resign at the end of this year and get a job somewhere else.

The thought of getting a job somewhere else or of going back to the classroom occurs to many new APs. The underlying question nags them: Is being an administrator worth it?

Despite all of these emotional burdens and sometimes disturbing reactions, most new assistants would say yes. It's an old joke, but one of the APs said he felt like the guy hired to follow the elephants around at the circus: He complained that all he ever saw was their back ends, he was often sprayed with unpleasant substances, and he did what was surely the most menial work in the troupe. But when someone finally asked him why he didn't quit, he answered: "What? And leave show business?"

"I like it," another new assistant told us, but she could not tell us exactly why. "I just do. It's in here [pointing to her head] and in here [pointing to her heart]."

One of the greatest rewards for many beginning assistants is the newfound camaraderie they feel with other administrators. It counterbalances and more than compensates for the negative feelings they have about the job. One man summed up the feelings of many:

It sounds silly to say, but this is the first time I've ever felt like a real part of a group at school. And it's because of what we go through together. Let me give you an example. We had a food fight in the cafeteria, and all of us had to go in to break it up and sort out who was responsible for what. Nothing, right? No, something. We still talk about it, laugh about it. We compare things to it. We share it. It's ours. I love it. I had great moments teaching, but nobody saw them. I could tell about them, but it sounded like bragging. You have to work a dance or a game and be in dark corners together to become a team.

Camaraderie affects attitudes and influences behavior. Personal commitment to the job, to comrades, and to their own performance affects new assistants. Many new APs do not feel as free to miss work as they had in their previous positions, explaining that they realize the increased burden it places on the other assistants and staff members. They indicated that they feel much more of a team involvement as APs than they felt in their prior positions and are surprised at the feelings they experience when they are away from the job. A woman told us:

I don't feel as free to be absent as I did when I was a teacher. There's no sub for an AP. I don't feel the freedom to take off personal necessity days. I worry that things are worse at work because I'm not there. The others have the burden of the whole school. I even felt guilty about having surgery and missing time.

Finally, a man told us:

You're going to think I'm crazy for saying this, and don't tell my wife, but after all the things I've told you, I like it. The truth is, I love it. I don't like certain of the parts, but I love the whole thing. This is a great bunch to work with, and we're all shoveling the shit together.

This sense of team pulls most new APs through the tough times and helps restore perspective when they most need it. Interestingly, most of the APs we talked with saw their experience shape up along a U curve. At the top when they begin the job, they are excited by their success, new status, and the belief that they really can make the difference they had been told they could by those who had trained them and hired them. Then school begins. The weight and pace of the job and the denial of expected opportunities to exercise instructional leadership take their toll. Most are anxious, uncertain, and feel overwhelmed and disappointed. At the same time, however, they begin to identify the bright spots and satisfactions that ultimately will sustain them in their decision to stay in administration. By spring, they become increasingly optimistic and confident, and by the end of the year, the vast majority say they can no longer picture themselves going back to the classroom.

Organizational socialization research is pointing more and more toward the entry experience as a series of overlapping experience stages of different durations for different individuals (Feldman, 1981, 1989; C. D. Fisher, 1986), and it clearly takes some people longer to become comfortable and effective in new situations than it does others. Unfortunately, adjustments beyond the first year are beyond the scope of this book. It has to suffice to assume that the odds are that, with more time, most will accommodate themselves to the job's demands. Perhaps the best indication we have that most new APs ultimately will benefit from their experience is, first, that more of the new assistants with whom we spoke reported more positive changes in themselves than negative, and second, that the vast majority felt pretty good about themselves by the end of the first year.

Even with all of the job's problems and pressures, most said they found the job invigorating. They knew the apparent contradiction in being simultaneously tired and invigorated but explained that the tiredness was the result of accumulated pressures. Even when they were tired, they were not bored. The greatest strength of the job, as one man put it, was:

There is always something going on, and most of the time it's new. Maybe in 3 or 4 years, I'll have seen it all, but right now, I never know what's coming, and I like it. Teaching was a routine. There isn't any routine here. Look at that phone. The few times I used it when I was a teacher, the subject was always the same: Johnny did this or Susie isn't doing that. And when I'd get a call, it was always the same: Can't you help Johnny with this? I know Susie's bright, but she just doesn't try. Now, I never know who is calling or why—well, almost never, and when I call, I never know the kind of response I'll get. It's exciting.

A young single woman explained how she sees herself and the change her family sees in her:

> My energy level is higher. I'm much more interested in life, [I have] a renewed interest in life. My brother comments that it's really neat to see me excited by what I'm doing. I expected to be worn out by the job. I thought I'd give it my all but I'd drag myself home. There are a couple of nights when I do go to sleep pretty early, but emotionally it's been unbelievably invigorating. Just great. And I'm afraid that it will wear off.

Invigoration is often attended by feelings of greater maturity, confidence, and professionalism. Among the new APs with whom we spoke, one delight is in the new sense of self they develop. A feeling of increased maturity is common and manifests itself in a greater ability to remain calm in the face of insult and attack, or as one man put it: "I've developed a thicker skin than I ever expected to." A woman described her feelings:

> Some things come up that maybe I'm not so concerned about as I was before. My daughter says, "I'm glad to see that you're laughing about it now." Maybe it's not all that important. Before, you thought if somebody told you where to go, that was the worst thing they could do, but I mean, now you just kind of take it in stride. And we've been cussed by the best of them, I guess. I think it's been a surprise to me that I can just take it in stride. I mean, as a teacher, you weren't looked at that way as much as you are as an administrator. And if you find your name written in different places in school, as a teacher, you would get wild. Now it's "Oh? Again?"

An AP for discipline displayed a sense of humor in echoing the remarks of the administrator above. At his school, he said:

> If you don't make the bathroom graffiti around here, it means you're not doing your job. That's been the measure for years on this campus. You know what really irritates me, though?

The graffiti never says that I get anything from anybody. I'm always just giving it!

Increased confidence, professionalism, and maturity also seem to show themselves in dress and demeanor:

Now I dress in ties and suits, and it tends to make me feel more professional. I notice a lot of times, instead of dressing in jeans like before, I might be dressed up at an event in a nice shirt and a tie. And I carry myself differently now. I think I was a confident person before, but I think it's even given me more confidence in what I'm doing. I like that feeling of introducing myself as an AP or someone introducing me by saying, "Well, this is [name]. He's an assistant principal at the high school." I think that's a nice feeling. Before, not that I was ashamed of being a teacher, but there's so many teachers out there. I enjoyed being a teacher, but this job is good for my ego. I've become more professional. I've become more mature.

Increased professional assertiveness is a common development in new APs. Part of the reason is because it is expected of them, but part of it is because they are more confident and believe they have ideas of value to contribute. A woman told us:

I was stagnating in teaching and didn't really know it, I guess. I would go to meetings, and I wouldn't say much. I felt like I could tell you anything you wanted to know about Spain and Mexico, teaching Spanish, and most anything Spanish, but that was it. Now I can see Spanish as one part of the program that is one part of the whole school. I'm always trying to assess how things fit together and influence each other in the school. Spanish is good for this school, especially with the kind of kids we have here, but it isn't the school. There's so much more, and this would be such a better place if I could get people to see that there is so much beyond their own classroom.

A high school AP told us the same thing from a different perspective:

When I was a teacher, I got appointed to a visiting accreditation committee for another school. It was a grueling 3 days, but it was wonderful. By the time it was over, I felt like I would be friends with my teammates forever, and I had learned so much. When I came back to my school, I wanted to change a lot of things and try the stuff I'd seen at the school where I'd gone. I was excited. I think that's one thing that drew me into administration. Now I'm in a constant accreditation. We're always evaluating something, and I'm always looking for new ideas. It's great. A lot of the stuff I had in my university classes makes sense, and I want to learn more. I don't have time to go to school now, but I want to try out these ideas.

Professional growth in new APs also often results in greater personal assertiveness. Dealing with discipline, of course, requires more assertiveness than dealing with compliant students. But dealing professionally with adults also requires more assertiveness, especially when teachers do not acknowledge the AP's expertise. "If I hear again," one woman told us, "that I have forgotten what it's like in the classroom or that I don't know anything about how to teach their subject, I may do murder."

In some instances, perhaps nature seeking a balance for the problems new APs take home, an increase in personal assertiveness has a positive effect on some home relationships: "My wife says she has seen an assertive side of me come out that she had never seen before—and she *likes it!*"

An important part of the growth process for many new assistants is both unexpected and a fitting way to close our profile of the typical first-year experience. It is particularly useful because it helps explain how a series of surprises, shocks, upsets, and frustrations can combine to produce a positive experience and promote growth.

Most of this book has catalogued and illustrated the surprises visited upon new APs as they begin their administrative careers. Whether pleasant or unpleasant, these surprises are unsettling; they go against both experience and expectation, and they require adjustment. Meryl Louis (1980) wrote a paper on the nature of surprises, in which she asserts that newcomers to a job always carry erroneous assumptions about their own skills, needs, and desires. These errors of self-expectation emerge when they encounter reality and are forced to recognize that their self-image is different from the one they held before taking the position. Louis argues that people usually think of unmet expectations as undermet expectations. But that is not necessarily the case. Every bit as surprising, and frequently as demanding of personal adjustment, are expectations that are overmet. Most new APs have this experience, and it ultimately overshadows all others: After being buffeted and battered by all manner of unfamiliar demands and situations, they rise to the occasion. The revelation of unexpected competence and understanding is wonderfully rewarding and fulfilling.

The true surprise for most is that this sense of accomplishment and ability most often derives from encounters for which neither their training nor their experience prepared them. New APs repeatedly told us that the satisfactions they had expected to draw from their new positions often were not the ones they actually drew. They talked about feeling as though their horizons had been expanded. They discovered that they can derive satisfaction from both more and different things than they had ever anticipated or previously felt.

An example from an AP in charge of guidance and attendance was representative of the surprise many feel. It is representative both because it illustrates that the surprise only emerged on reflection and because the satisfactions she describes were among the most commonly reported:

> It's a lot less student contact than I had imagined, and I miss that. And the student contact is different. It's usually that you're asserting your authority in very difficult, touchy situations. It's not the same satisfaction you get from the counseling relationship.
>
> I thrive on challenges. I mean, I like the unexpected. I like things to be different each minute, each day. I don't like routine. So I guess the satisfaction I get out of the job is feeling that I have responded appropriately or creatively to the things that come up.
>
> This was a surprise. I expected my major satisfaction would be in working with the staff and helping them move from Point A to Point B and then addressing the needs of the changing

student body. As we worked together as a team, I would see satisfaction in that. Actually, that's turned into frustration! [laughs] The satisfaction is that I am a wonderful problem solver for problems I never knew existed!

Another woman's feelings were also representative:

Look, I can do this. When I was offered this job, I told a friend that I was really scared of it. It seemed like such a responsibility, and the potential was there for so much conflict. I didn't know if I could handle it. She asked me a question that really made me think. She's not in education, but she said, "Are the people who are doing it now so much smarter than you? Do you think they have some kind of magic?" I told her I didn't. I think I maybe even was a little indignant about it. But I think the truth is that I did think that. There's a mystique about power. I always thought the people in the office knew best. I didn't think I could do what they could do, but I guess I had to find out. And I can.

Perhaps the best example given us was the AP described above who had to deal with the deaths of six students during the course of his first year in office. In reflecting on this experience, he drew together the elements that undergird the positive experience of the AP: competence, confidence, and camaraderie in a moving environment that won't even stop for death in its ranks.

If I had been told beforehand that this was going to happen, I would have doubted that I could handle it—both in terms of administrative skills and emotions. I was surprised that I was able to rise to the occasion. I was overwhelmed at times, and I wondered what I had gotten myself into, but I had little time really to dwell on my feelings. I realized that all eyes were turned on the principal and me, expecting us to provide stability in an unstable situation. It helped to know that I didn't have to handle these situations alone. Working closely with the principal in responding to the events resulted in a very strong sense of camaraderie between the principal and me. I do reflect, now, on the very troubled lives so many of our students endure and how little we can do to help.

Providing "stability in an unstable situation" defines an essential role played by APs and, by underscoring unpredictability, helps explain why it is so difficult to prepare newcomers for the job. The experiences of the new APs with whom we spoke suggest that the challenges, conflicts, pace, emotional upheavals, and competing demands that form their first year create a crucible from which they can—but do not always—emerge stronger both personally and professionally. As Henry James (1922, p. viii) observed:

No themes are so human as those that reflect for us, out of the confusion of life, the close connection of bliss and bale, of the things that help with the things that hurt, so dangling before us forever that bright hard medal, of so strange an alloy, one face of which is somebody's right and ease and the other somebody's pain and wrong.

Taken by Surprise

Draw from others the lesson that may profit yourself.
Terence, *Heauton Timoroumenos*

A poster marketed by the Leanin' Tree Publishing Company shows the face of a grizzled old cowboy. He looks weathered, intense, formidable, not very happy, but not quite angry. Beneath the picture, a line reads: "There were a helluva lot of things they didn't tell me when I hired on with this outfit." The caption could be a new AP's theme.

We first saw the poster framed and hanging in an AP's office in southern California. In the course of our conversation, he pointed to it and said it summed up his first year exactly. For him, and for most of the new assistants with whom we talked, the first year as an administrator was filled with "a helluva lot of" surprises that provided living examples of what research tells us about the nature of transition.

Transitions, whether in the larger context of life in general or in the specific context of work, have two distinguishing characteristics. The first is a sense of discontinuity: recognition that today is not the same as yesterday. The second is a forced development of new behavioral responses in order to cope with today's reality (Hopson & Adams, 1977; Schlossberg, 1981).

148

Everyone handles the details of his or her personal and professional transitions in an individual way, but organizational research has revealed common themes in work transitions as people struggle to make sense of the new situation. People work to develop a clear picture of the role to be played, the context in which it is to be performed, and the web of relationships that both surround and connect it to other parts and operations of the organization. In the process, they come to redefine themselves in terms of the role and undergo a series of personal, as well as professional, adjustments.

There is no way to completely prepare for a work transition. Every transition involves some element of surprise, simply because not everything about a job or about what emotional reactions it will elicit are knowable in advance. At the same time, however, the number of surprises and the burdens of adjustment can be reduced to the extent that newcomers can become aware of what the job entails, know its potential opportunities and frustrations, and have a sense of the skills and behavioral responses it commonly requires for successful performance.

At least seven tasks are involved in successfully completing a work transition: (a) be initiated to the work group; (b) be initiated to the job, master its technical requirements; (c) develop a frame of reference to measure how and why things are done as they are; (d) learn who the important players are; (e) define roles for oneself within the work and social groups of which one now is a part; (f) learn to deal with varieties of conflicts—role, intergroup, personal; and (g) learn to manage the job in relation to life outside of work (Feldman, 1976a, 1976b, 1981; Louis, 1982; Nicholson & West, 1988).

Ideally, newcomers arrive on a job knowing what it is about and trained to deal with the challenges it commonly presents. More often in the assistant principalship, they arrive knowing little or nothing about the job and suffer a difficult transition because of the overwhelming amount to learn on the job. Worse, many new APs come to the job with inappropriate training and misconceptions about what they will be called on to do. To build from ignorance is difficult, but it is less psychologically taxing and time consuming than to start with inappropriate knowledge and clear expectations that are patently wrong. Expecting one thing and consistently encountering another requires new APs to unlearn, or at least set aside, their misconceptions, adjust to the real situation, and learn what is needed to successfully engage it as it unfolds. As one man told us, he felt like he had to "build the boat and row it at the same time."

The experiences of new APs imply that many come into office knowing little or nothing of the job and laboring under serious misconceptions of what the assistantship is about; these fall under four broad themes. New APs consistently report that (a) the nature of the office was a surprise to them, (b) they were not trained in the skills they needed to perform effectively, (c) they were not sharpening their skills to become a principal, and (d) they were unprepared for the impact the job had on them professionally and personally.

Themes in the Stories New Assistant Principals Tell of Their First-Year Experiences

Theme 1: Most Beginning APs Do Not Understand the Nature of the Assistant Principalship

This theme was the most common message coming through the conversations we had with the new APs, and it is small wonder that most go into the office knowing little and harboring unrealistic expectations. The structure and operation of secondary schools, the emphasis in most university credential programs, and the focus of educational research combine to conceal the nature of the office.

Concealed by School Structure. The assistant principalship is difficult for most secondary school teachers to observe because of school structure. Isolated in their classrooms, teachers have limited interaction with colleagues and supervisors, especially compared with professionals in other fields (Boyer, 1984; Davis, 1987; Lieberman, 1985; Sizer, 1984). They generally know little about what happens in school outside their own classrooms (Corcoran, 1990; Feiman-Nemser & Floden, 1986). Teachers' involvement with other adults often is restricted to rushed lunch hours, occasional breaks, meetings, and the parking lot. Although teachers work in the same building with administrators and are affected by administrative decisions, few ever get a close, sustained look at the many activities that make up an AP's day.

Ironically, the more efficient and effective administrators are, the more their activities are invisible to teachers because they buffer the classroom from interruption. Without a reason to look, teachers do not see the processes of administration that surround them.

Administrative actions are accepted by teachers as a matter of course, drawing attention only when something is left undone or goes wrong. Teachers know that certain students are present in class, for example, but do not know they are there because an administrator counseled, cajoled, conspired, and coordinated efforts with parents and community authorities. Teachers know administrators deal with students sent to the office, but typically know little about the preemptive steps taken to quell potential problems before they can interfere with classroom instruction. Teachers expect the building to have light, heat, books, and materials, and that the assembly, dance, meeting, athletic contest, or graduation will come off smoothly. They see the results but not the behind-the-scene planning and effort.

Teachers also have little opportunity to observe the dynamics of administrator problem-solving behavior. They receive minutes of meetings or summaries of actions taken with students, but the interactions and processes leading to operational decisions or to problem resolution cannot adequately be captured and conveyed in brief reports. The myriad duties APs routinely handle are not observable from the classroom, even in schools that involve teachers in site management. While teachers rightly focus their attention on their classes, administrators invisibly undertake dozens of other tasks that maintain the school's infrastructure. The work APs do becomes fully visible to teachers only when they become administrators.

Concealed by Administrator Preparation Programs. Earning an administrative credential at a university usually does not improve a teacher's understanding of the assistant principalship. None of the new APs we spoke with had the opportunity to take a university-level course on the subject or ever used a text that considered the office unique and valuable.

AP experience is not incorporated into university curricula, and APs are all but ignored in administrative textbooks. In 1984, Gorton surveyed all of the universities belonging to the University Council on Educational Administration (UCEA) and found none that offered courses on the assistant principalship (Marshall, 1992). His respondents believed that courses for principals would be adequate for assistants.

We reviewed 20 textbooks used in initial certification programs and found the expected emphasis on the principalship. Texts rarely mention the assistant principalship, and we could find no works that gave particular attention to its unique qualities. In a review of the graduate catalogues of more than 80 universities, we could find no courses on the assistant principalship and no indication that courses on the principalship explore the special qualities of the assistant's office.

The assistant principalship seems invisible to universities. As a result, students are given the erroneous impression that duties, leadership demands, and opportunities for APs are little different from those of the principal.

Concealed by the Research Literature. The educational administration literature also gives little attention to APs. Journals designed for teachers, of course, rightfully concentrate on the problems, opportunities, and techniques of the classroom. Administrative research literature, however, reflects the failure of universities to recognize the assistant principalship as a distinct and important position. Perusal of the ERIC system or the periodical stacks in any university library reveals the comparative inattention given APs. Even two of the major administrative research compendia virtually ignore the office. *The Handbook of Research on Educational Administration* (Boyan, 1988) does not list the assistantship in either its table of contents or index, mentioning it in only one article, in which it is characterized as a location on the career path to higher office. *The Encyclopedia of School Administration and Supervision* (Gorton, Schneider, & Fisher, 1988) does not include the assistant principalship in its discussion of school administration roles.

Theme 2: New APs
Often Lack Needed Skills

Aspiring administrators understandably believe that their studies have prepared them for the challenges they will face. After they actually begin their jobs, however, they are surprised to find that they have few opportunities to exercise the kind of leadership they thought was typical of principals and at the heart of the job. Instead of being able to concentrate on curriculum, teaching, and learning, they must cope with things unplanned and for which they had no training (Eades, 1983; Smith, 1984).

Even though the positions share similar titles, an assistant principalship is not a smaller version of a principalship, and new APs quickly learn that job realities are defined by functions, not by titles. The realities of the offices are different because they sit on different tiers in the authority structure. Although often overlooked in leadership studies, the hierarchical level of a job has a defining influence on its nature, significantly affecting attitudes, behaviors, and leadership practices (Pavett & Lau, 1983; Pelz, 1951; Yukl, 1994). First-level leaders—those at the top—face responsibilities and challenges different from those of second-level leaders. The more elevated the position in the hierarchy, the more complex the decision making (Martin, 1959).

First-level leaders are "boundary spanners" who, more than anyone else in the building hierarchy, must give their attention both to the interplay of groups within the organization and to the organization's links with the external environment (Aldrich & Herker, 1977; Leifer & Huber, 1977). They must think in holistic terms, understand the complexities of the system, know how to develop and articulate a vision, and know how to motivate others to contribute to its fulfillment (Bennis & Nanus, 1985; Rosenbach & Taylor, 1993). Schein (1992) argues that creating organizational culture through the definition and inculcation of broad-based beliefs may be the only really important thing top leaders do.

In contrast, the primary task of second-level leaders, such as APs, is to implement the visions of those who lead them (Barnard, 1938; Niles, 1949, 1958) by breaking major, long-term organizational concepts and goals into smaller, incremental components. As goals are operationalized into specific tasks and as those tasks are delegated down the structure, objectives and responsibilities become increasingly specific (Barnard, 1938). Mastery of technical details is more valuable to lower level leaders than to upper level ones (Badawy, 1988). Knowing discipline code and attendance law specifics, for example, is more valuable to the AP than to the principal, just as subject expertise is more valuable to the classroom teacher than to the AP.

Specific short-range objectives generate a variety of immediately demanding tasks. Time lines are shorter at this level of the hierarchy, and the work is more often managerial, aimed at stabilizing the organizational environment (Pfiffner & Sherwood, 1960). Second-level leaders must react quickly to real and perceived threats of disruption, which necessarily makes their work more reactive than proactive. They tend to perceive their disturbance-handling and system-negotiating roles as more important than any they may have in long-range planning and development, and they have more difficulty than their superiors in controlling their time (Austin & Brown, 1970; Mintzberg, 1973; Pavett & Lau, 1983; Pellicer et al., 1988; Staff, 1988). These conditions mark a decided contrast with both what they experienced in the classroom and what they were led to expect in administration.

Typically, an AP's workday resembles Mintzberg's (1973) classic description of managerial activity: a great deal of work, done at an unrelenting pace in an unpredictable environment of stimulus and response, characterized by variety, fragmentation, and brevity. The wide variety of AP responsibilities has been confirmed in many studies (e.g., Austin & Brown, 1970; Glanz, 1994; Hentges, 1976; Marshall, 1992, 1993), and a very clear picture is found in a study Pellicer and his associates (1988) did for the National Association of Secondary School Principals (NASSP).

Pellicer and associates identified, in priority order, the degree of responsibility APs have for particular responsibilities:

1. Handling of student discipline
2. Administration of school policies
3. Evaluation of teachers
4. Special arrangements
5. Student attendance
6. Graduation activities
7. Emergency arrangements

8. Building use—school related
9. New student orientation programs
10. Student assemblies
11. Teacher duty rosters
12. Administrative representative
13. School master schedule
14. School dances
15. Instructional methods
16. Orientation programs for new teachers
17. Faculty meetings
18. Substitute teachers
19. School calendars
20. Curriculum development

Their list illustrates two important points about the assistant principalship: (a) The responsibilities are wide ranging and (b) few provide opportunities for long-range planning or visionary leadership.

The responsibilities of APs are unrelenting and unpredictable, as well as variable, and they require attention every day the school is open. APs can plan time for teacher observations and conferences, curriculum development, and brainstorming, but they cannot predict when events will require immediate response and cause them to abandon their plans. Staff members expect APs to give immediate attention to problems such as instructional material supply, heating and cooling systems malfunction, safety concerns, and interpersonal disputes—especially student discipline (Jeter, 1993; Pellicer et al., 1988; Reed & Himmler, 1985).

The dimension of immediacy in so much of an AP's work explains why Mintzberg's notions of brevity and fragmentation are descriptive of an assistant's day. APs often find it impossible to see a task through to completion; they must leave it to attend to some other planned or emergent responsibility, which, in turn, is interrupted by something else. Because many staff members in secondary schools are available only between classes or during short breaks, most interactions with them are necessarily brief. As a result, APs often can spend only a short time working on any one thing, in marked contrast with when they were teachers. The time management techniques they studied in their principal preparation programs do not work in this environment.

Shared responsibility and authority in the assistant principalship also contribute to the fragmentation of APs' experience. Assistants rarely have full responsibility for any particular task. They usually share duties and accountability with other staff members (Pack, 1987; Patton, 1987; Pellicer et al., 1988). This means shared authority and poses another challenge. APs cannot issue orders to peers who occupy what Sayles (1979) calls "side-ways relationships." They must work with and through others to accomplish tasks, a difficult and time-consuming process requiring heavy investment in lateral communication and persuasion.

The ability to influence peers and subordinates is necessary, but APs also must influence those above them in the hierarchy in order to acquire the resources and authority they need to influence peers and subordinates. The need to continually influence those above them is not a part of an AP's training because the unspoken assumption is that, as leaders, they are already at the top of the hierarchy— which APs are not. Still, research has demonstrated that leaders who are able to influence their own superiors also have more influence with their followers (Graen, Cashman, Ginsburgh, & Schiemann, 1978; Pelz, 1951, 1952). To meet their own obligations and coordinate the implementation of policy, new APs must learn what can be gotten from whom and how to get it (Katz & Kahn, 1966). Lacking the authority of upper hierarchical positions, they must develop the skill to build power bases, establish the right connections, and maintain a positive and productive relationship with the boss (Austin, 1988).

The difference between the roles and responsibilities of principals and APs is not lost on subordinates, to the distress of new assistants who expected to have final authority in at least some areas of their work. Principals are perceived as leaders by staff members; APs, although a step removed from the staff, are seen as also directed by the principal. Principals have an immediate presence in the building and usually have final responsibility for faculty and staff evaluations. They can initiate direct interaction with others; in fact, the administrative leadership literature encourages it (e.g., Blumberg & Greenfield, 1986; Donaldson, 1991; Peters & Waterman, 1982). This action strengthens the principal's position as leader, but it reduces the assistant's by encouraging direct-line communication with top authority (Nealey & Fiedler, 1968). As a result, APs are not perceived as building or campus leaders, so the possibility of being bypassed or overridden always exists—something with which principals rarely must contend.

Training for APs needs to reflect these realities. We have neither space nor need here to make specific recommendations for an AP curriculum. The purposes of this book were descriptive, and the outlining of a corrective course of study is beyond its scope. Nonetheless, the new AP stories illustrate that they have an immediate and continuing need for conflict resolution skills, legal knowledge, counseling skills, communication skills, and skills of persuasion. Yet only a few of the APs with whom we spoke ever had a class in discipline administration, and those who had reported that the course was focused more on classroom management than on campuswide discipline. Fewer yet had formal instruction in conflict resolution, performance appraisal feedback techniques, detection of deception, counseling techniques, effective conduct of meetings, specific techniques of making public presentations, or administrative communications. None had ever had training in working with a secretary or other classified personnel.

Theme 3: The Assistant Principalship Does Not Prepare an AP for the Principalship

One of the enduring myths of the assistant principalship is that it is a training ground for principals (Kelly, 1987), but the new APs' stories we heard and the research on veteran APs refute the claim (Glanz, 1994; Golanda, 1993-1994; Greenfield, 1984; Greenfield et al., 1986; Kelly, 1987; Koru, 1993). Because the tasks of each are so different, experiences in the assistantship are likely to distort a new AP's professional development and blunt the growth of commitment to educational improvement (Greenfield et al., 1986).

The process of organizational socialization frequently is described in three stages (Buchanan, 1974; Porter, Lawler, & Hackman, 1975; Wanous, 1980): (a) a period of anticipatory socialization in which expectations about the job and about what the person will be like in the job are developed through imagination, observation, experience, and education; (b) an entry and encounter period in which the newcomer meets the reality of the position and begins the process of adjustment; and (c) a stabilization or role-management period in which integration into the organization and the integration of the work into life outside the organization is achieved.

The entry and encounter stage is the testing of professional and personal expectations. Research indicates that the encounter period may be the most critical socialization stage because attitudes that will affect later development are generated then (Berlew & Hall, 1966; Buchanan, 1974; Nicholson & West, 1988). Part of socialization is formal preparation, but research shows that a stronger force is on-the-job experience, and educational research specifically demonstrates that administrators learn the job while in it (Heller, Conway, & Jacobson, 1988). Socialization theory predicts, and research supports the idea, that new administrators will "take the role as given, accept the status quo and assume a caretaker response to the responsibilities, missions, and activities associated with the role" (Greenfield, 1985, p. 110).

The nature of the assistant principalship and the skills required to be successful as an AP are oriented much more toward management than toward leadership, a condition that does not promote the development of visionary leadership in its occupants (Glanz, 1994; Greenfield, 1984; Greenfield et al., 1986; Kelly, 1987; Koru, 1993). Working continually to stabilize the school environment, APs tend to adopt a custodial orientation (Van Maanen & Schein, 1979) that reduces the odds of later becoming a principal who will effectively pursue beneficial change in the institution. Instructors in their credential programs attempt to teach them the leadership skills the instructors want them to have for tomorrow's schools, which they must then put into a professional deep freeze while they learn the way schools operate today, with the hope that they can resurrect their visionary education sometime later when they become principals (Schein, 1987). Marshall (1992, p. 110) believes that the office holds the potential for this stultifying effect on even the strongest of people: "Gandhi, Jane Addams, and Martin Luther King would not have survived assistant principalhood; moving into higher leadership would have been out of the question" because the practice of the office cripples an individual's ability to think like a critical humanist.

Theme 4: Becoming an AP Brings Professional and Personal Changes

The fourth theme in the new AP experience is their lack of preparation for what the job may do to them professionally and personally, though they learn quickly that the assistant principalship can have a powerful effect. They can no longer see schools and schooling as they did from the classroom. Their new perspective forces them to reconceptualize their notions of secondary schools and to create a cognitive map into which they must place the relative positions of important organizational features and the roles of important people (Van Maanen, 1977). The task also requires them to redefine and locate themselves in the context of the organization as they now perceive it. This requirement sometimes involves a personal, as well as professional, reassessment.

Recognizing the New Perspective. Some new APs, with no forewarning through experience or preparation, find it difficult to abandon the assumptions and measures they used successfully for years in the classroom and to alter their perspectives on secondary schooling. Teachers and administrators do not use the same kinds of information to determine success and failure, assess status and progress, and make decisions.

Mitchell and Spady (1977) characterize the teacher's perspective on schools and schooling as *transformational* and the administrator's as *stabilizing*. Teachers focus on transforming individual students through instruction and guidance. Thinking in terms of the single student, they measure a student's grades, a student's behavior, and a student's graduation. Administrators concentrate on stabilizing the organization and creating an environment conducive to the transformational activities undertaken by the teachers as a group. The caliber of administration is measured by the quantity and quality of the transformations accomplished over time. Consequently, administrators most often think in aggregate terms: grade distributions, mean achievement scores, referral rates, and graduation/dropout rates.

Tension can build between transforming and stabilizing activities. Individual expressions clash with organizational norms; professional prerogatives clash with state and board mandates. As transformers, teachers pursue classroom autonomy for themselves and encourage individual student growth and expression. As stabilizers, administrators work with groups to ensure consistency and coordination. In the administrative view, curriculum alignment, sequential learning, and discipline codes require convergent behavior from teachers and students, rather than divergent behavior and accommodation of individual preference. How these conflicts are perceived and resolved is important to all (McNeil, 1988), but especially to administrators who control authority and bear overall responsibility for teacher and student performance.

In terms of administrative socialization, the successful transition from teacher to administrator requires one to perceive the operation of a school from the stabilizing perspective, a change often difficult for teachers who have prided themselves on making independent professional decisions and attending to individual student differences. They are now called on to carry out collective administrative priorities and experience an internal conflict because the settings and issues are the same but the focus is different, and it is difficult to build new responses to familiar stimuli in familiar settings (Brett, 1984; Hopson & Adams, 1977; Jones, 1983).

Redefining Roles. Redefining roles and fixing them in the context of the organization is a difficult task for any newcomer but is especially so for new APs who have not been schooled to understand either their roles or the multiple and conflicting expectations others hold for them. The expectations people hold for teachers are spread across a narrower band and are less conflicting than those they hold for administrators. As a result, new APs experience an inevitable increase in conflict and an escalation of stress beyond what they felt as teachers.

New APs frequently do not realize how many groups hold expectations for administrators and how many of them may conflict. The AP's behavior can influence students, parents, the faculty, the support staff, administrators in other schools and the district office, the school board, employees of other districts, and social and public agencies.

Teachers expect that the AP will back them when their professional judgment is challenged by parents or students. Administrators

viewed as consistently siding against teachers violate this expectation and eventually lose the respect and support of the faculty. At the
same time, students expect justice and assistance, and parents expect
APs to be their advocates when they or their children raise what they
consider to be legitimate concerns, especially when the consequences
are severe for their students. Principals expect APs to loyally carry
out administrative policies; classified staff members often turn to
APs when others make unreasonable demands or are disrespectful;
and community agencies expect APs to conform to their policies and
practices.

Not all role difficulties derive from attempts to satisfy the expectations of others. New APs also are surprised to find role conflicts
built into the structure of the job. It is very difficult, for example, to
simultaneously be a sounding board or confidant for employees and
still be responsible for their evaluation. Another example is the
tension between excellence and efficiency when assigning teachers
outside their areas of expertise because the master schedule will not
work any other way or in recommending teachers of lesser academic
talents for employment because they also can coach. Role conflicts
are not limited to the school site. New APs put more time into their
jobs than do teachers, are involved in more stressful situations, and
are away from home more often. As a result, they face conflicts in
which the role of spouse or parent competes with the work role.

An AP's work has a high potential for conflict, a fact that has
several important implications for those who assume the job. First,
as Cuban (1989) observes, conflict is the DNA of school administration; it is inevitable and pervasive. Second, conflict resolution is
rarely straightforward and reasonable. Conflict interactions are sustained by the often unpredictable moves and countermoves of participants, who consciously and unconsciously are driven by a wide
range of variables (Folger, Poole, & Stutman, 1993). Third, APs frequently must make decisions more on the basis of intuition than on
fact and often are unable to predict how others will react. Administrative decisions can have important consequences for others, and
new APs can spend sleepless nights wrestling with the relative merits
of decisions they can neither feel comfortable with nor avoid making.

Teachers expect that, as APs, they can settle differences to everyone's
satisfaction by employing the kindness and carefully developed sense

of fairness they used so successfully in the classroom, but they often are shocked by others' reactions. Regardless of their good intentions and responsiveness, APs make decisions that anger others and sometimes engender continuing enmity.

Considering the stress of settling conflicts among individuals who hold differing views of appropriate behavior, it is easy to see how adjustment to multiple role expectations can contribute to promotion trauma. Role theorists contend that administrators' behavior can be shaped by their perceptions of how others want them to behave (Yukl, 1994). Role conflict and stress result when conflicting demands are placed on them. The level of stress depends on the number of people making demands and the degree to which the expectations of those people are incongruent (Gross, Mason, & McEachern, 1958). In situations with multiple and incongruent demands, the perspectives, values, and responses built up over years of experience as teachers engaged in transformational activities come into conflict with the new responses required by an organizational perspective.

How new assistants respond to the expectations of various groups is an interesting and personal process. Managers appear to be influenced by three types of factors in making their decisions: structural, social, and individual (Tsui, 1994). *Structural factors* include not only such elements as the reward system and the distribution of power among employees but also the extent to which goals are either shared or conflicting among the constituents in the organization. These elements determine the levels of independence and interdependence that people feel when establishing their priorities. *Social factors* include group norms, how personally and socially similar to the decision maker are those wanting support, and the level of trust among individuals and groups in the organization. *Individual factors* include the characteristics of the individual decisionmaker's personality, ability, and motivation. Confronting the varying shapes of each of these factors and their contributing elements and facing up to which are driving forces in their individual value systems often cause new APs to reassess their personal as well as professional priorities. The results of the analysis can be surprising.

A clear message runs through the stories that first-year APs tell of their experiences. When new APs hold state- and university-approved credentials but consistently report that they entered the assistant principalship without knowledge of its purpose and limitations, without the skills they need to perform effectively, and without realizing the professional and personal impact it might have on them, the implication is evident: There is a terrible mismatch between the training new APs are given and the jobs they assume.

Afterword

This book is intended for multiple audiences: students in educational administration credential programs; students, teachers, classified employees, and parents that APs serve; school principals who supervise credential students during their field practicums; district personnel who hire new APs and the administrators who induct and supervise them; university faculty who design and implement credential programs in educational administration; and those interested in reforming schools.

Students in Administrative
Preparation Programs

Credential students are our primary audience. We hope this book will provide aspiring administrators who will serve as secondary school APs with a realistic picture of the position that awaits them.

Although one might wish that the duties of assistant principals in schools would be restructured so that APs would have more opportunities to exercise educational leadership, the reality in many cases is that APs will not be spending their time supervising instruction, developing the school's curriculum, or engaging in long-range planning. Their days, instead, will be filled handling a disparate array of responsibilities and attending to the seemingly endless problems that walk through their doors. The pace and unpredictability of the job will stretch their tolerance and sap their reservoir of confidence. They will experience the conflicting emotions of fatigue and energy, sorrow and humor, disappointment and success. Some will discover that administration is not for them; others will find it exhilarating and fulfilling. We hope that if new APs enter the job with a realistic understanding of the position, they can better serve the schools to which they are assigned.

Those Whom the
Assistant Principal Will Serve

As noted earlier, the full range of the AP's responsibilities and the demands made on APs remain largely invisible to most who come into contact with them. Each group—teachers, classified staff members, students, and parents—sees APs from a unique perspective and often fails to see the overall picture of the job. We hope this book will give the teachers and classified staff members who work directly with the APs, and the students and teachers with whom APs interact, some understanding and appreciation for the complex and important role APs play in the operation of schools.

School Administrators
Who Supervise Credential
Students During Their Field Practicums

Virtually all administrative credential programs include some form of field practicum that requires students to spend time working with a participating principal or AP in a school setting. The range, duration, and intensity of field practicums differ considerably among administrative credential programs. Some require students to invest a substantial amount of time at one or more school sites; others demand far less, allowing students to free up an hour here and there from their teaching responsibilities to work on projects in the principal's office or to observe and talk with principals about their work. The APs we spoke with, when evaluating their preparation, listed the field practicum as the most important and meaningful part of the program.

Given the complexities of the AP's job and the power of apprentice-type programs, one would hope that field practicums would be as demanding and extensive as possible and that those who supervise credential students would create realistic pictures of the principalship and the assistant principalship while providing honest feedback to students about their administrative potential.

District Personnel Who Hire
First-Year Assistant Principals
and Principals Who Supervise

Regardless of the intensity and effectiveness of their credential preparation programs, newly hired APs have a great deal to learn during their first year on the job. Many new APs have had, at best, limited exposure to a few facets of the job. If their experiences during their first year are similar to those of the first-year APs with whom we spoke, they will be surprised by the scope, pace, and intensity of the job. They increasingly will be isolated from their former teaching colleagues, and they often will hesitate to share their insecurities or concerns with the supervising principals who evaluate their performance.

It is critically important that school district personnel and supervising principals recognize the challenges newly hired APs face and provide opportunities for them to receive continued support, instruction, and mentoring. New APs need time to reflect informally with other new administrators about their experiences. The first year on the job is rich with "teachable moments," and supervising principals can have a significant and lasting impact on the development of new administrators.

Those Who Design and Implement Administrative Credential Programs

Being an AP in today's secondary schools is serious business and deserves serious consideration in administrator training. APs often find themselves in physical, emotional, and legal situations that are potentially damaging. Through administration of discipline alone, many are called on to conduct searches, confront intruders, deal with weapons and drug offenses, engage in substance abuse counseling and suicide prevention, counsel adolescents and their families, and deal with a wide range of community agencies, especially the police. To send graduates into that world without adequate preparation is irresponsible. University faculty in credential programs must take whatever steps are necessary to ensure that admitted students have high administrative potential and are realistically prepared.

Others Interested in Improving Today's Secondary Schools

Many legislators, business leaders, academics, civic leaders, parents, and citizens have expressed their concerns about secondary schools, and many are engaged in activities and programs to make the schools better. Seymour Sarason (1971) reminds us that we cannot hope to improve the schools without first coming to understand them as they actually are, not as we might think or hope they are. This book's descriptions of the challenges APs encounter provides a window through which those outside education can gain a better understanding of the complexities and challenges faced in today's secondary schools. Fights that used to be settled with fists are now, too often, settled with weapons; the traditional challenges of tobacco and alcohol use have been augmented, even eclipsed, by powerful and deadly drugs; the traditional sexual concerns of pregnancy and venereal disease have been overshadowed by the finality of AIDS; and families that used to be allies in solving problems are now too often part of the problem. Employees, students, and parents are much quicker to take their conflicts with school officials to court. Society's powerful forces have breached the walls of our schools and have made the task of school reform infinitely more complex. No plan for improving schools can succeed unless it accounts for these realities.

Finally, we believe that those who read this book will gain, as we did in writing it, a clearer understanding of the difficult tasks facing APs and a deeper appreciation of the important role they play in today's schools. To be prepared, new APs must know what lies ahead; to be effective, they must be trained to meet it.

A Few Words About the Data

Two simultaneously produced data sources provided the foundation for this book. The first was a personal diary kept by an associate during her first year as an assistant principal in a junior high school. Much of its contents are personified by the character of Maria Winston in Chapter 1. The second was a collection of narratives gathered as part of a dissertation research study at UCLA (Hartzell, 1990) that explored the initial socialization experiences of 21 first-year APs in high schools. As dissertations are required to be, that study was formal, theory-based, and systematic.

We were intrigued that two such disparate documents essentially described the same experiences: the surprise and challenge of adjusting to a new status and environment, learning to deal with new perceptions of time, mastering discipline, redefining or creating relationships with coworkers, and feeling the impact of the job at a personal level. To follow our interest, we augmented the narratives we had with stories we collected from APs we knew and met. In fact, collecting new AP stories became something of an avocation among us. Another source of narratives developed when the third author became an AP and shared her experiences. The more induction tales we gathered, the more they confirmed the diary and the dissertation and the clearer it became that common experiential threads existed that did not receive adequate attention in educational administration literature.

We all lived in California, but eventually one of us moved to Washington and another to Nebraska. We remained interested in new APs, however, and continued to pool and compare the experiences we gathered from beginning administrators. In 1992, we realized that we had amassed a collection of interesting and, more important, instructive stories. We decided to write a book and purposefully sought information to confirm or deny what we now understood to be the experience of new APs. Our jobs provided ideal opportunities to do so: One of us is a high school AP and the other two are university professors teaching in administrator preparation programs.

Between 1992 and mid-1994, we arranged three ways to interact with new APs in California, Nebraska, and Washington. First, during the 3 years, approximately 40 new APs in three cohorts, each made up of assistants in their first year in office, accepted invitations to attend periodic meetings at one of the universities. These sessions were, in effect, confidential support groups for new APs, held with the expressed purpose of allowing beginning assistants to compare experiences and to discover that they were not alone. They proved a rich source of confirmatory information. The participants experienced the same feelings that Maria had recorded in her diary and that dissertation informants had contributed.

University students pursuing additional certification and doctoral degrees in educational administration provided another source of information. Practicing first-year secondary school APs were encouraged to describe their experiences.

A final source was developed by the author who served as an AP. She had opportunities to meet with other new assistants in the course of her work, at professional organization meetings and in university classes she took to fulfill the second level of administrator education required under California credentialing laws. Again, stories from her counterparts and colleagues reflected the themes identified in this book.

Although this sample is not completely representative of those usually associated with formal, scientifically designed studies, it does have some elements of deliberate design. Maria's diary is a case study in socialization, and the 21 new APs studied in the dissertation were selected to represent various groups and settings. The remaining informants were engaged as a convenience sample, often self-selected. This book, however, is not a large-scale study of those who go into the assistant principalship. Instead, it tries to capture feelings in context. Those who shared their experiences included personal and professional characteristics sufficiently diverse, we believe, to support an exploratory study of individual impressions of professional change and personal transition. Our guiding belief is that the sampling participants told us the truth about their experiences, which are spread across enough differing environments with enough variables to suggest high odds that most new APs will encounter something similar.

Greene and David (1984) assert that representation of every possible variable is not needed among subjects in a study. It is sufficient if a substantive reason can be given to include a particular combination. The responsibility in qualitative research is to select informants who vary enough among themselves to represent a spectrum that is relevant to understand the concern under study (Patton, 1990). We believe that our sample meets those criteria. Using the dissertation sample, the diary, our own experiences, and the experiences that others shared with us, we drew information from new APs who included males and females; Whites, Blacks, Hispanics, and Asians; persons whose ages ranged from 26 to early 50s; single, married, and divorced persons, with and without children; former teachers, counselors, deans, and activity directors from both high schools and junior highs; people who became administrators in their own schools, and others who changed schools, districts, and/or levels to take their new positions; people who worked for principals of the same or differing race and/or gender; some from schools as small as 600 or as large as 3,500; persons working in urban, suburban, and rural schools, with high, middle, low, and mixed socioeconomic standing; and persons working in schools dominated by an ethnic or racial group or with a mixture.

Because the APs were assured anonymity, no details were included that could suggest a location or identity. The greatest adaptation of data was the material contained in Maria's diary in Chapter 1.

The adequacy of data representations in a descriptive work should be judged in relation to its purpose (Dawson, 1982, p. 2). Accepting this premise, our responsibility is to convince the reader that our descriptions and conclusions are trustworthy. *Trustworthy* does not mean the same thing as *valid* in the terminology of experimental studies. Rather, it means that the results of the study are as accurate as they can be in the given circumstances.

Guba (1981, p. 80) believes that the "truth value" in a study like this is determined by "testing the credibility of their findings and interpretations with the various sources (audiences or groups) from which data were drawn." His recommendation is to do "member checks," asking members of the human data source group to render opinions of accuracy and comprehensiveness.

We did a variety of member checks. First, the dissertation had four member checks built into it: (a) review of transcribed conversations by the 21 participating informants to validate that their remarks had been accurately recorded; (b) a survey administered to the 21 participants, fashioned from the information they had individually provided; (c) presentation of the findings to administrators in a school district from which none of the 21 participants had come but that included 11 administrators who either were current APs or who had held that post within the preceding 10 years; and (d) a review by seven personal friends, all of whom had been APs at one time. In every case, the members considered the findings congruent with their experience.

In many ways, the AP meetings at the university and the discussions with practicing APs in university classes, at professional meetings, and in workplace interactions constituted a second series of member checks even though some of these conversations supplied additional data in the form of stories.

A third member check was to ask three current and three former APs to read the book manuscript and comment on it. They all thought it was consistent with their experience.

A fourth check was not exactly a "member" check except in an indirect sense. We compared the stories the new APs told us with the descriptions of AP life to be found in the small AP research literature. We found nothing in conflict with the major themes in that literature. Actually, we found the reverse: The stories the APs told us could be used to illustrate much of what is described elsewhere in administrative research.

Qualitative research is locked into contextual boundaries. We represent this book only as a realistic look at a complex, uncharted world. A single glance is not enough to see everything, however, and further research—impressionistic, qualitative, and quantitative—will be required before we can develop the richly detailed picture of the AP's world that we have of the teacher's world that new assistants leave behind.

References

Aldrich, H. E., & Herker, D. (1977). Boundary spanning roles and organizational structure. *Academy of Management Review, 2*(2), 217-230.

Ancell, B. M. (1988). *Role of the assistant principal in junior high/middle schools in the state of Illinois.* Unpublished doctoral dissertation, Southern Illinois University, Carbondale.

Argyris, C., & Schon, D. A. (1974). *Theory in practice: Increasing professional effectiveness.* San Francisco: Jossey-Bass.

Ashford, S. J., & Cummings, L. L. (1983). Feedback as an individual resource: Personal strategies of creating information. *Organizational Behavior and Human Performance, 32*(3), 370-398.

Austin, D. B., & Brown, H., Jr. (1970). *Report of the assistant principalship: Vol. 3. The study of the secondary school principalship.* Washington, DC: National Association of Secondary School Principals.

Austin, M. J. (1988). Managing up: Relationship building between middle management and top management. *Administration in Social Work, 12*(4), 29-47.

Badawy, M. K. (1988). Why managers fail. In R. Katz (Ed.), *Managing professions in innovative organizations* (pp. 162-169). New York: Ballinger.

Baker, K. (1985). Research evidence of a discipline problem. *Phi Delta Kappan, 66*(4), 482-496.

Barnard, C. (1938). *The functions of the executive.* Cambridge, MA: Harvard University Press.

Bauer, G. L. (1985). Restoring order to the public schools. *Phi Delta Kappan, 66*(4), 488-491.

Bennis, W., & Nanus, B. (1985). *Leadership: The strategies for taking charge.* New York: Harper & Row.

Berlew, D. E., & Hall, D. T. (1966). The socialization of managers: Effects of expectations on performance. *Administrative Science Quarterly, 11*(2), 207-223.

Blumberg, A., & Greenfield, W. (1986). *The effective principal: Perspectives on school leadership* (2nd ed.). Boston: Allyn & Bacon.

Boyan, N. J. (1988). *The handbook of research on educational administration.* New York: Longman.

Boyer, E. L. (1984). *High school: A report on secondary education in America.* New York: Harper & Row.

Brett, J. M. (1984). Job transitions and personal and role development. In K. M. Rowland & G. R. Ferris (Eds.), *Research in personnel and human resources management: A research annual* (Vol. 2, pp. 155-185). Greenwich, CT: JAI.

Brown, J. J. (1985). *The role of the Georgia high school assistant principal as perceived by principals and assistant principals.* Unpublished doctoral dissertation, University of Georgia, Athens.

Buchanan, B. (1974). Building organizational commitment: The socialization of managers in work organizations. *Administrative Science Quarterly, 19*(4), 533-546.

Butler, J. K. (1983). Reciprocity of trust between professionals and their secretaries. *Psychological Reports, 53*(2), 411-416.

Campbell, R. F., Fleming, T., Newell, L. J., & Bennion, J. W. (1987). *A history of thought and practice in educational administration.* New York: Teachers College Press.

Carlson, R. O. (1964). Environmental constraints and organizational consequences: The public school and its clients. In D. E. Griffiths (Ed.), *Behavioral science and educational administration: The 63rd yearbook of the National Society for the Study of Education, Part II* (pp. 262-276). Chicago: National Society for the Study of Education.

Carona, C. W. (1986). *The role of assistant principals in large high schools in Texas.* Unpublished doctoral dissertation, University of North Texas.

Center for Education Statistics. (1987). *Public school teacher perspectives on school discipline.* Washington, DC: U.S. Department of Education.

Center for Public Interest Polling. (1986). *The New Jersey school teacher: A view of the profession.* New Brunswick, NJ: Eagleton Institute.

Clark, C. M., & Peterson, P. L. (1986). Teachers' thought processes. In M. C. Wittrock (Ed.), *Handbook of research on teaching (3rd ed., pp. 255-296). New York: Macmillan.*

Corcoran, T. B. (1990). Schoolwork: Perspectives on workplace reform in public schools. In M. W. McLaughlin, J. E. Talbert, & N. Bascia (Eds.), *Contexts of teaching in secondary schools: Teachers' realities* (pp. 142-166). New York: Teachers College Press.

Corwin, R. G., & Borman, K. M. (1988). School as workplace: Structural constraints on administration. In N. J. Boyan (Ed.), *The handbook of research on educational administration* (pp. 209-238). New York: Longman.

Cuban, L. (1986). Principaling: Images and roles. *Peabody Journal of Education, 63*(1), 107-119.

Cuban, L. (1989). The district superintendent and the restructuring of schools: A realistic appraisal. In T. J. Sergiovanni & J. H. Moore (Eds.), *Schooling for tomorrow: Directing reforms to issues that count* (pp. 251-271). Boston: Allyn & Bacon.

Curwin, R. L., & Mendler, A. N. (1988). *Discipline with dignity.* Alexandria, VA: Association for Supervision and Curriculum Development.

Davis, J. B. (1987). Teacher isolation: Breaking through. *High School Journal, 70*(2), 72-75.

Dawson, J. A. (1982, March). *Qualitative research findings: What do we do to improve and estimate their validity?* Paper presented at the Annual Meeting of the American Educational Research Association, New York. (ERIC Document ED 218 330)

Donaldson, G. A., Jr. (1991). *Learning to lead: The dynamics of the high school principalship.* Westport, CT: Greenwood.

Doyle, W. (1986). Classroom organization and management. In M. C. Wittrock (Ed.), *Handbook of research on teaching* (3rd ed., pp. 392-431). New York: Macmillan.

Duane, E. A., Bridgeland, W. M., & Stern, M. E. (1986). The leadership of principals: Coping with turbulence. *Education, 107*(2), 212-219.

Duke, D., & Stiggins, R. (1988). *The case for commitment to teacher growth: Research on teacher evaluation.* Albany: State University of New York Press.

Dwywer, C. P. (1994). *Administrator perceived differences in the role of the suburban secondary school assistant principal.* Unpublished doctoral dissertation, Temple University, Philadelphia.

Eades, S. L. (1983). *The high school assistant principalship: Present and ideal roles and needed changes.* Unpublished doctoral dissertation, University of Maryland, College Park.

Eidell, T. L. (1965). *The development and test of a measure of the pupil control ideology of public school professional staff members.* Unpublished doctoral dissertation, Pennsylvania State University, University Park.

Emmer, T. E. (1981). *Effective classroom management in junior high mathematics classrooms* (Research and Development Report No. 6111). Austin: University of Texas Research and Development Center for Teacher Education.

Emmer, T. E. (1984). *Classroom management: Research and implications* (Research and Development Report No. 6178). Austin: University of Texas Research and Development Center for Teacher Education.

Emmer, T. E., & Evertson, C. M. (1981). Synthesis of research on classroom management. *Educational Leadership, 38*(4), 342-347.

Feiman-Nemser, S., & Floden, R. E. (1986). The cultures of teaching. In M. C. Wittrock (Ed.), *Handbook of research on teaching* (3rd ed., pp. 505-526). New York: Macmillan.

Feldman, D. C. (1976a). A contingency theory of socialization. *Administrative Science Quarterly, 21*(3), 433-452.

Feldman, D. C. (1976b). A practical program for employee socialization. *Organizational Dynamics, 5*(2), 64-80.

Feldman, D. C. (1981). The multiple socialization of organization members. *Academy of Management Review, 6*(2), 309-318.

Feldman, D. C. (1989). Careers in organizations: Recent trends and future directions. *Journal of Management, 15*(2), 135-156.

Feldman, D. C., & Arnold, H. J. (1983). *Managing individual and group behavior in organizations.* New York: McGraw-Hill.

Ferris, G. R., & Kacmar, K. M. (1988, March). *Organizational politics and affective reactions.* Paper presented at the 30th Annual Meeting, Southwest Division of the Academy of Management, San Antonio, TX.

Fisher, C. D. (1986). Organizational socialization: An integrative review. In K. M. Rowland & G. R. Ferris (Eds.), *Research in personnel and human resource management: A research annual* (Vol. 4, pp. 101-145). Greenwich, CT: JAI.

Fisher, D. C. (1986). *Organizational newcomers' acquisition of information from peers.* Unpublished doctoral dissertation, Yale University, New Haven, CT.

Folger, J. P., Poole, M. S., & Stutman, R. K. (1993). *Working through conflict: Strategies for relationships, groups, and organizations* (2nd ed.). New York: HarperCollins.

Glanz, J. (1994). Redefining the roles and responsibilities of assistant principals. *The Clearing House, 67*(5), 283-287.

Gmelch, W. H., & Swent, B. (1984). Management team stressors and their impact on administrators' health. *Journal of Educational Administration, 22*(2), 192-205.

Golanda, E. L. (1993-1994). The assistant principalship: Is it a dysfunctional role that may also be an impediment to restructuring? *National Forum of Educational Administration and Supervision Journal, 10*(2), 37-51.

Gorton, R., Schneider, R. A., & Fisher, J. C. (1988). *The encyclopedia of school administration and supervision.* Phoenix, AZ: Oryx.

Graen, G. B., Cashman, J. F., Ginsburgh, S., & Schiemann, W. (1978). Effects of linking-pin quality upon the quality of working life of lower participants: A longitudinal investigation of the managerial understructure. *Administrative Science Quarterly, 22*(3), 491-504.

Greene, D., & David, J. L. (1984). A research design for generalizing from multiple case studies. *Evaluation and Program Planning, 7*(1), 73-85.

Greenfield, W. D. (1984, April). *Sociological perspectives for research on educational administrators: The role of the assistant principal.* Paper presented at the Annual Meeting of the American Educational Research Association, New Orleans. (ERIC Document ED 249 623)

Greenfield, W. D., Jr. (1985). The moral socialization of school administrators: Informal role learning outcomes. *Educational Administration Quarterly, 21*(4), 99-119.

Greenfield, W. D., Marshall, C., & Reed, D. B. (1986). Experience in the vice principalship: Preparation for leading schools? *Journal of Educational Administration, 24*(1), 107-121.

Gross, N., Mason, W. S., & McEachern, A. W. (1958). *Exploration in role analysis.* New York: John Wiley.

Guba, E. G. (1981). Criteria for assessing the trustworthiness of naturalistic inquiries. *Educational Communication and Technology: A Journal of Research and Development, 29*(2), 75-91.

Hartzell, G. N. (1990). *Rookie year: The on-the-job surprises of first-year public high school assistant principals.* Unpublished doctoral dissertation, University of California, Los Angeles.

Heller, R., Conway, J., & Jacobson, S. (1988). Executive educator survey. *Executive Educator, 10*(9), 18-22.

Hentges, J. T. (1976). *A normative study of the assistant principalship in selected Minnesota secondary schools.* Unpublished thesis, Mankato State University, Mankato, MN.

Hopson, B., & Adams, J. D. (1977). Towards an understanding of transition: Defining some boundaries of transition. In J. Adams, J. Hayes, & B. Hopson (Eds.), *Transition: Understanding and managing personal change* (pp. 1-71). Montclair, NJ: Allenheld & Osmun.

Hoy, W. K. (1965). *Dogmatism and the pupil control ideology of public school professional staff members.* Unpublished doctoral dissertation, Pennsylvania State University, University Park.

Jablin, F. M. (1984, May). *The assimilation of new members into organizational communication systems: A longitudinal investigation.* Paper presented at the Annual Convention of the International Communication Association, San Francisco.

James, H. (1922). *What Maisie knew.* London: Macmillan.

Jeter, A. L. (1993). *Assistant principals and principals: A national comparison of perceptions about duties and responsibilities.* Unpublished doctoral dissertation, University of South Carolina, Columbia.

Johnson, S. M. (1990). The primacy and potential of high school departments. In M. W. Mclaughlin, J. E. Talbert, & N. Bascia (Eds.), *The contexts of teaching in secondary schools: Teachers' realities* (pp. 187-223). New York: Teachers College Press.

Jones, G. R. (1983). Psychological orientation and the process of organizational socialization: An interactionist perspective. *Academy of Management Review, 8*(3), 464-474.

Jung, C. (1923). *Psychological types.* New York: Harcourt Brace.

Katz, D., & Kahn, R. L. (1966). *The social psychology of organizations.* New York: John Wiley.

Keedy, J. L. (1991). *School improvement practices of successful high school principals.* West Carrollton: West Georgia Regional Center for Teacher Education.

Kelly, G. (1987). The assistant principalship as a training ground for the principalship. *NASSP Bulletin, 71*(501), 13-20.

Koppich, J., Gerritz, W., & Guthrie, J. W. (1986). *A view from the classroom: California teachers' opinions on working conditions and school reform proposals.* Palo Alto, CA: Policy Analysis for California Education.

Koru, J. M. (1993). The assistant principal: Crisis manager, custodian, or visionary? *NASSP Bulletin, 77*(556), 67-71.

Kounin, J. S. (1970). *Discipline and group management in classrooms.* New York: Holt, Rinehart & Winston.

Latane, B. (1981). The psychology of social impact. *American Psychologist, 36*(4), 343-356.

Leifer, R., & Huber, G. P. (1977). Relations among perceived environmental uncertainty, organizational structure, and boundary spanning behavior. *Administrative Science Quarterly, 22*(2), 235-247.

Lieberman, A. (1985). Why we must end our isolation. *American Teacher, 70*(1), 9-10.

Louis, M. R. (1980). Surprise and sense making: What newcomers experience in entering unfamiliar organizational settings. *Administrative Science Quarterly, 25*(2), 226-251.

Louis, M. R. (1982). Managing career transition: A missing link in career development. *Organizational Dynamics, 10*(4), 68-77.

Louis, M. R., Posner, B. Z., & Powell, G. N. (1983). The availability and helpfulness of socialization practices. *Personnel Psychology, 36*(4), 857-866.

Marshall, C. (1992). *The assistant principal: Leadership choices and challenges.* Newbury Park, CA: Corwin.

Marshall, C. (1993). *The unsung role of the career assistant principal.* Reston, VA: National Association of Secondary School Principals.

Martin, N. H. (1959). The levels of management and their mental demands. In W. L. Warner & N. H. Martin (Eds.), *Industrial man:*

Businessmen and business organizations (pp. 276-294). New York: Harper.

McLaughlin, M. W., Talbert, J. E., & Bascia, N. (Eds.). (1990). *The contexts of teaching in secondary schools: Teachers' realities.* New York: Teachers College Press.

McNeil, L. M. (1988). Contradictions of control: Part 1. Administrators and teachers. *Phi Delta Kappan, 69*(5), 333-339.

Mechanic, D. (1962). Sources of power of lower participants in complex organizations. *Administrative Science Quarterly, 7*(3), 349-364.

Metropolitan Life. (1986). Metropolitan Life survey of former teachers in America, 1986. *American Educator, 10*(2), 34-39.

Mintzberg, H. (1973). *The structure of managerial work.* New York: Harper & Row.

Mitchell, D. E., & Spady, W. G. (1977, April). *Authority, interaction, processes, and functional task structures in the school.* Paper presented at the Annual Meeting of the American Educational Research Association, New York.

Mobley, W. H. (1982). Supervisor and employee race and sex on performance appraisals: A field study of adverse impact and generalizability. *Academy of Management Journal, 25*(3), 598-606.

Moles, O. C. (Ed.). (1990). *Student discipline strategies: Research and practice.* Albany: State University of New York Press.

Nealey S. M., & Fiedler, F. E. (1968). Leadership functions of middle managers. *Psychological Bulletin, 70*(5), 313-329.

Nicholson, N., & West, M. (1988). *Managerial job change: Men and women in transition.* Cambridge, England: Cambridge University Press.

Niles, M. C. (1949). *Middle management: The job of the junior administrator.* New York: Harper.

Niles, M. C. (1958). *The essence of management.* New York: Harper.

Ortiz, F. L., & Marshall, C. (1988). Women in educational administration. In N. J. Boyan (Ed.), *The handbook of research on educational administration* (pp. 123-141). New York: Longman.

Pack, S. R. (1987). *A profile of the high school assistant principal in Georgia.* Unpublished doctoral dissertation, University of Georgia, Athens.

Patton, J. (1987). *The role and function of assistant principals in Virginia senior high schools.* Unpublished doctoral dissertation, Virginia Polytechnic Institute and State University, Blacksburg.

Patton, M. Q. (1990). *Qualitative evaluation and research methods* (2nd ed.). Newbury Park, CA: Sage.

Pavett, C. M., & Lau, A. W. (1983). Managerial work: The influence of hierarchical level and functional specialty. *Academy of Management Journal, 26*(1), 170-177.

Pellicer, L. O., Anderson, L. W., Keefe, J. W., Kelly, E. A., & McCleary, L. E. (1988). *High school leaders and their schools: Vol. 1. A national profile.* Reston, VA: National Association of Secondary School Principals.

Pelz, D. C. (1951). Leadership within a hierarchical organization. *Journal of Social Issues, 7*(3), 49-55.

Pelz, D. C. (1952). Influence: A key to effective leadership in the first-line supervisor. *Personnel, 29*(1), 3-11.

Peters, T. J., & Waterman, R. H., Jr. (1982). *In search of excellence.* New York: Harper & Row.

Peterson, K. D. (1977-1978). The principal's tasks. *Administrator's Notebook, 26*(8), 4-8.

Pfiffner, J. M., & Sherwood, F. P. (1960). *Administrative organization.* Englewood Cliffs, NJ: Prentice Hall.

Pondy, L. R. (1967). Organizational conflict: Concepts and models, *Administrative Science Quarterly, 12*(2), 296-320.

Porter, L. W., Lawler, E. E., & Hackman, J. R. (1975). *Behavior in organizations.* New York: McGraw-Hill.

Rafilides, M., & Hoy, W. K. (1971). Student sense of alienation and pupil control orientation of high schools. *High School Journal, 55*(3), 101-111.

Ralston, D. A. (1985). Employee ingratiation: The role of management. *Academy of Management Review, 10*(3), 477-487.

Reed, D. B., & Himmler, A. (1985). The work of the secondary vice principal. *Education and Urban Society, 18*(1), 59-84.

Rosenbach, W. E., & Taylor, R. L. (Eds.). (1993). *Contemporary issues in leadership* (3rd ed.). Boulder, CO: Westview.

Sarason, S. (1971). *The culture of school and the problem of change.* Boston: Allyn & Bacon.

Sayles, L. (1979). *Leadership: What effective managers really do and how they do it.* New York: McGraw-Hill.

Schein, E. H. (1987). Organizational socialization and the profession of management. In E. H. Schein (Ed.), *The art of managing human resources* (pp. 101-117). New York: Oxford University Press.

Schein, E. H. (1992). *Organizational culture and leadership* (2nd ed.). San Francisco: Jossey-Bass.

Schlossberg, N. K. (1981). A model for analyzing human adaptations to transition. *Counseling Psychologist, 9*(2), 2-18.

Shulman, L. S. (1989). Teaching alone, learning together: Needed agendas for the new reforms. In T. J. Sergiovanni & J. H. Moore (Eds.), *Schooling for tomorrow: Directing reforms to issues that count* (pp. 166-187). Boston: Allyn & Bacon.

Siskin, L. S. (1991). Departments as different worlds: Subject subcultures in secondary schools. *Educational Administration Quarterly, 27*(2), 134-160.

Sizer, T. (1984). *Horace's compromise.* Boston: Houghton Mifflin.

Smith, J. A. (1984). *A comparative study of the role of the secondary assistant principal: New demands, new realities, and new perspectives.* Unpublished doctoral dissertation, Seattle University, Seattle, WA.

Staff, S.A.B. (1988). *A study of the responsibilities and authority of the high school assistant principal as perceived by principals and assistant principals.* Unpublished doctoral dissertation, University of Michigan, Ann Arbor.

Stohl, C. (1986). The role of memorable messages in the process of organizational socialization. *Communication Quarterly, 34*(3), 231-249.

Stoner, L. H., & Voorhies, W. T. (1981). The high school assistant principalship in NCA schools in Indiana. *North Central Association Quarterly, 55*(4), 408-413.

Stumpf, S. A., & London, M. (1981). Capturing rater policies in evaluating candidates for promotion. *Academy of Management Journal, 24*(4), 752-766.

Sue, D. W., & Sue, D. (1990). *Counseling the culturally different: Theory and practice.* New York: John Wiley.

Terkel, S. (1970). *Hard times.* New York: Pantheon.

Terkel, S. (1974). *Working.* New York: Pantheon.

Terkel, S. (1984). *The good war.* New York: Pantheon.

Tsui, A. S. (1994). Reputational effectiveness: Toward a mutual responsiveness framework. In B. M. Staw & L. L. Cummings (Eds.), *Research in organizational behavior: Vol. 16. 1994* (pp. 257-308). Greenwich, CT: JAI.

Ubben, G. C., & Hughes, L. W. (1992). *The principal: Creative leadership for effective schools* (2nd ed.). Boston: Allyn & Bacon.

Van Maanen, J. (1977). *Organizational careers: Some new perspectives.* New York: John Wiley.

Van Maanen, J., & Schein, E. H. (1979). Toward a theory of organizational socialization. In B. M. Staw (Ed.), *Research in organizational behavior* (Vol. 1, pp. 209-264). Greenwich, CT: JAI.

Wanous, J. P. (1980). *Organizational entry: Recruitment, selection, and socialization of newcomers.* Reading, MA: Addison-Wesley.

Weick, K. E. (1979). *The social psychology of organizing* (2nd ed.). Reading, MA: Addison-Wesley.

Weick, K. E., & McDaniel, R. R., Jr. (1989). How professional organizations work: Implications for school organization and management. In T. J. Sergiovanni & J. H. Moore (Eds.), *Schooling for tomorrow: Directing reforms to issues that count* (pp. 330-355). Boston: Allyn & Bacon.

Wheeler, S. (1966). The structure of formally organized socialization settings. In O. G. Brim & S. Wheeler (Eds.), *Socialization after childhood* (pp. 53-116). New York: John Wiley.

Williams, J. M. (1979). *Relationship of organizational climate and socioeconomic status to pupil control behavior.* Unpublished doctoral dissertation, University of Kansas, Lawrence.

Williams, M. (1972). *The pupil control ideology of public school personnel and its relationship to specified personal and situational variables.* Unpublished doctoral dissertation, University of Georgia, Athens.

Willower, D. J., Eidell, T. L., & Hoy, W. K. (1967). *The school and pupil control ideology* (Penn State Studies, No. 24, 1st ed.). University Park: Pennsylvania State University.

Willower, D. J., Eidell, T. L., & Hoy, W. K. (1973). *The school and pupil control ideology* (Penn State Studies No. 24, 2nd ed.). University Park: Pennsylvania State University.

Willower, D. J., & Jones, R. G. (1963). When pupil control becomes an institutional theme. *Phi Delta Kappan, 45*(2), 107-109.

Wilson, B., & Corcoran, T. (1988). *Successful secondary schools: Visions of excellence in American public schools.* East Sussex, England: Falmer.

Yinger, R. J. (1979). Routines in teacher planning. *Theory Into Practice, 18*(3), 163-169.

Young, I. P. (1982). A multivariate study of administrator leadership behavior and custodial satisfaction. *Planning and Changing, 13*(2), 110-123.

Yukl, G. (1994). *Leadership in organizations* (3rd ed.). Englewood Cliffs, NJ: Prentice Hall.

Index